In Charge: Managing Money for Christian Living

IN CHARGE

Managing Money for Christian Living

LEE E. DAVIS

BROADMAN PRESS
Nashville, Tennessee

©Copyright 1984 • Broadman Press
All Rights Reserved
4264-04
ISBN: 0-8054-6404-2
Dewey Decimal Classification Number: 332-024
Subject Headings: FINANCE, PERSONAL // BUDGETS, HOUSEHOLD //
STEWARDSHIP
Library of Congress Catalog Number: 84-4969
Printed in the United States of America

Scripture quotations unless otherwise indicated are from the
New American Standard Bible. Copyright © The Lockman Foundation, 1960, 1962,
1963, 1968, 1971, 1972, 1973, 1975, 1977. Used by permission.

Scripture quotations marked KJV are from the
King James Version of the Bible.

Library of Congress Cataloging in Publication Data

Davis, Lee E., 1938-
  In charge.

  Includes bibliographical references.
  1. Finance, Personal—Religious aspects—
Christianity. I. Title.
HG179.D35   1984   332.024'2   84-4969
ISBN 0-8054-6404-2 (pbk.)

To Sarah,
whose companionship, participation,
and support have made Christian management
more of a reality in our home;
And to Cindy, Eddie, and Kellie
who had to wait for Dad and Mom to learn
about Christian Management.

In Appreciation

I thank all of my colleagues at the Stewardship Commission of the Southern Baptist Convention who encouraged me, read the manuscript, and made many valuable suggestions for this book. Special thanks go to Ernest Standerfer, director of Stewardship Development and my supervisor, who gives me freedom to be as creative as I'm capable of being and in many unique ways made it possible for me to do this writing.

I also thank the state Stewardship and Cooperative Program directors and associates of the state Baptist conventions with whom I'm privileged to work. They, too, have made a great contribution to my ministry and to the writing of this book.

CONTENTS

CONTENTS

Prologue
A Personal Pilgrimage

God created all of the nonhuman world, then created human beings, and placed us *in charge*. God's revelation of himself in Christ further clarified what he expects each of us to do in and with his world. The basic expression of our relationship to God's material world and to the people of the world is the way we manage our money and the goods and services which money can buy.

I was a pastor when I first began studies which eventually led me to make a commitment to practice Christian money management. Just out of seminary and wanting to be an effective pastor, I was looking for ways to expand the church's ongoing ministries and respond to special ministry opportunities. The need for stewardship development in the church seemed obvious.

Since I knew so little about stewardship, I began to do some research—Bible study in particular. After I started studying, I realized I didn't even know as much as I had thought. The studies and resulting stewardship programs did produce amazing results for the church. Within eighteen months, giving had increased 47 percent and mission giving had almost tripled. But my personal money management was not improved at this point. My family's life-style continued unchanged.

From my studies, I discovered that the word *steward* in the Bible means "manager," and *stewardship* means "management." These meanings are significant to me now in understanding Christian money management. At first, however, I only used the ideas for preaching on giving. I was more interested in increasing the giving level of church members than helping them, and myself, develop a Christian lifestyle. It's the depth of meaning contained in the biblical words *manager* and *management* that has changed my life and ministry.

In this book, the familiar definition of the words *manage* and *management* are relevant but enlarged to emphasize the unique Christian application. In a dictionary, to manage is to have charge of; direct; to handle or use carefully. Management is skillful handling; executive ability. For Christians, such actions are in response to God. This is what makes Christian management distinct from other management responses. It's at the level where we live—daily decisions and choices about the use of money—that God's design for money management enriches our lives.

Personal Reflections

When I first started sharing how Christian money management had changed my life and family for the better, I was embarrassed. To illustrate the change, I had to share some of both my past and present financial activities. Unlike people in many countries of the world, most Americans appear to have difficulty revealing details about their personal finances. I'm more comfortable in sharing now because of the identification I've come to feel with so many other families whose mismanagement has created financial chaos, also.

To illustrate management and mismanagement, I'll reflect often upon some of my family's experiences. In doing so, I'm reminded of what the naturalist Thoreau wrote in *Walden:* "I should not talk so much about myself if there were anybody else whom I knew as well."[1]

Incomewise, my family was near average after twenty-one years of marriage. My wife and I had three healthy children, all older teenagers with the oldest in college. As more than 50 percent of all wives and mothers, my wife was employed outside of the home. Her employment was not by choice. With debts, a daughter in college, and two other children approaching college age, it seemed an economic necessity for survival.

The history of our mismanagement is somewhat typical. We began our marriage on the front end of the "buy now, pay later" boom in the late 1950s. We soon became addicted to having what we wanted before we could afford it. With my discharge from the air force, there followed sixteen years of college, seminary, and graduate school, along with part-time pastorates. The three children were born during the first six years of our marriage. We developed a pattern of financing our life with revolving credit. Spending decisions were mostly made on our ability to make increased monthly payments.

After twenty-one years, the financial legacy I had to leave my children was how to struggle from one payday to the next. To live as we did took some good rationalization. I reasoned that my family needed to dress reasonably well and drive a dependable car. And how could that be done on a pastor's salary without using credit?

I further rationalized that someday I would not be a student pastor, that I would have more income. Then I could manage my finances differently. When I became a full-time pastor, nothing changed. I now understand that an unhealthy emphasis on eventuality can short-circuit daily Christian growth, create meaningless life-styles, and jeopardize the future.

When conviction of our mismanagement came, it was from two directions. I was confronted with the biblical doctrine of stewardship (management). As the truth began to unfold, I realized that personal, daily money management could not be separated from my commitment to Christian living. As a Christian living in a country where money is so essential, I discovered that money management can be one of the most visible expressions of Christian commitment. In our economy, management is essential for maximum Christian witness. Management or the lack of it determines one's life-style. Mismanagement reduces or even prevents effective witness.

Conviction came to my wife from another direction about the same time. She had a strong commitment to mission ministries and was involved in the mission organizations of our church. Aware of the literacy mission work needing to be done in our city, especially with internationals and refugees, she wanted to give herself more fully to this volunteer mission work. She wanted to quit her job!

Our convictions complemented each other. After discussing our separate convictions, the similarity of each was apparent. I supplied her with the information on Christian money management which I had discovered. After she studied the material, together we made a recommitment to Christ which included Christian money management and the volunteer literacy mission work. It was a life-changing commitment.

It took contemplated commitment to a Christian life-style to change old mismanagement habits. But after we began to practice Christian money management, other beneficial changes were apparent. One change involved our relationship with the children concerning money. They were in high school and college. Behavioral experts say that by that age a person's basic life-style is rather fixed. We cautioned ourselves not to turn them off with a revival-like fervor. But our newfound contentment and peace of mind were apparently contagious. Their greater security was and is evident.

We worked at giving the children freedom to make management and spending decisions. That was a first around our house. We involved them in the family management plan. They made most of their own decisions about buying their personal things within the framework of the family budget we had agreed upon. The once frequent words *we can't afford it* disappeared. Not that suddenly we could afford whatever we wanted; we just chose not to think in those terms any longer. We began to plan for what we needed in order to make cash purchases.

Life-styles can be changed at any age when Christian commitment is involved. Practicing Christian money management can change basic patterns of living. For example, our craving for "things" was almost unconsciously reduced. Our lives became less complicated, simpler.

At the time of this writing, we're five years past that significant day when we made our life-changing commitment. The impact has been tremendous! I never realized how many hours a day I spent worrying about finances which are now used for more helpful purposes. The increased opportunities for mission support and personal involvement have exceeded our greatest expectations. We planned for my wife to become involved in local literacy mission work. She accomplished that, and she has been to West Africa three times for a total of twelve weeks teaching literacy.

My Concerns

I have indicated that I mismanaged my finances for many years, and that since beginning to practice Christian money management my financial status has improved greatly. But I have been careful to avoid the implication that Christian money management is only for those Christians having financial difficulties. The responsibility to practice Christian money management does not exclude a single Christian because of social or economic class.

Whether a person or family has millions, thousands, or hundreds of dollars does not change the management responsibility. All Christians at all economic levels have the same purpose: to use their lives, powers, influence, and resources to do those kinds of things in the world which God expects from his highest creation. This common purpose among Christians is reflected in the mission Christ gave to his church (Matt. 28:19-20).

Further, I can't accept the premise that God meant for his people to live in as much luxury as their resources will permit. This book should not be interpreted as offering a means for Christians to become materially prosperous for their own advantage. I have no desire to make a contribution to "Christian materialism." But I heartily accept the biblical truth that God's material creation is good, not evil, and wealth is a valuable asset in enlarging God's kingdom.

Still another concern involves motive. Within the freedom which God has given us, he trusts us to respond to him without manipulation and without external, predefined standards—including those for Christian giving. Your church is responsible for teaching you Christian stewardship (management). It is also right to expect you to give because giving is the nature of Christians. But your church should teach you Christian money management to help you grow as a disciple with no strings attached.

If you have not been practicing Christian money management and you do make a commitment to begin, your giving will likely increase. But the decision to increase your giving is between you and God. It's a matter of freedom and trust. God created us free to choose to love him.

What If?

What if my wife and I had made a commitment to Christian money management with several thousand dollars ahead rather than several thousand dollars in the red? Or what if we had come to this commitment with large and prosperous business holdings? Or what if we had an upper income salary and an investment portfolio which would create envy on Wall Street?

The joy and satisfaction would have been the same! Lifestyle changes would no doubt have been different but nonetheless welcomed! Similar contentment would have been experienced! The only difference would have been greater available resources to help enlarge God's kingdom and minister to people in need! Truly biblical: "From everyone who has been given much shall much be required; and to whom they entrusted much, of him they will ask all the more" (Luke 12:48).

In a Nutshell

Throughout the book, *principles of Christian money management* are inserted which relate to the material that follows them. It will become apparent that the bulk of the material falls under the first three principles. Look for these seven principles as you read.

1. God is owner.
2. Persons are managers.
3. The biblical doctrine of management shapes a Christian's life-style.
4. Our attitude influences our money management.
5. A commitment to biblical management prevents mismanagement.
6. Christian management guides our use of money and material things.

7. Adhering to the biblical management doctrine balances responsibility of planning for the future with responsibility for Christian ministries and family needs.

I like to compare Christian money management to a construction project. First, justification is needed—a reason why. If it's a building, the justification will likely be a specific need for a building, perhaps a family dwelling or a church building. Based on Bible study, I'm convinced that every Christian has a responsibility to practice careful money management. There are spiritual and moral reasons for it. When a project is justified, construction can be planned. But unlike the need for a building which may have an alternative—renting or leasing—I can find no such option for Christian money management in Scripture.

I have been guided on my pilgrimage in Christian money management by doctrine which produced commitment and practical life-style applications. However, I have not become the perfect manager. I am serious about becoming the best Christian manager humanly possible, so management is a conscious daily part of the routine of my life. The only Christians I know who are serious about money management are those who are still working at it.

Note

1. Henry David Thoreau, *Walden and Other Writings,* ed. Brooks Atkinson (New York: The Modern Library, 1937), p. 3.

Part
1

Biblical Concepts of Management

1

God's Assignment . . . Take Charge

Christian money management is supported in the Bible. It is based on one of the most visible biblical doctrines, the doctrine of stewardship. The word *stewardship* in the Bible is the translation of the Greek word *oikonomia*. It is the act of management. A steward (*oikonomos*) is a manager. To be a manager is to be assigned responsibility, to have oversight, to be in charge of something that belongs to another person.[1]

Most every person can identify with the management concept. The free enterprise system uses management principles extensively. Everyone in the system from the owner to the laborer understands what it means to be a manager, to be in charge of something that belongs to another person. Management is based on relationships. In its simplest form, there are three relationships: the owner relates to his property, the owner and manager relate to each other, and the manager relates to the owner's property. This triangle of management relationships was first established in creation between God, the world, and humanity.

PRINCIPLE ONE: **God is owner.**

Owners Give Management Assignments

We have no problem understanding the authority, privileges, and responsibilities that go with claiming ownership. In the county where I live, the courthouse has a record that I own a piece of property. Tax records show that there is a house located on the property. Since I "own" it, I have authority to sell it, lease it, rent it, or remove the house. Basically, unless I infringe upon my neighbors' rights and freedoms, I have authority to determine how the property is to be used, even to assigning the management of it to someone else.

Ownership by the Maker: God Created

God owns everything. This is a fact we need to consciously affirm because it determines so many of our attitudes and actions. Lest we forget, "God created the heavens and the earth" (Gen. 1:1). We recognize that the maker of a thing has authority over it. The maker has earned the right to enjoy the benefits of that which he makes. If we claim this right, it is even more true with God.

The secular laws of ownership which govern our right to use and enjoy property came to us from early Roman law. It developed out of conquest: one group of people who were able to conquer another displaced the first group and occupied their territory. We reflect this when we candidly say that "possession is nine-tenths of the law." We champion our legal laws of ownership because it gives us the right to use and enjoy our possessions. Also, it provides for basic human freedoms which include the ability to respond to God in worship through giving and ministry to others. However, this is not our greatest pride in ownership.

Our greatest pride in our concept of ownership is power,

the power to keep others from using and enjoying our possessions. For example, I have a deed which legally proves that I own property. But in what real way do I assert my ownership? By living in the house located on the property? Not really; that right goes unquestioned. The proof of ownership, and the pride of it, is in the fact that I have the legal power to prevent you from occupying the property.

Herein is the distortion and the tragedy: when we forget that God is the absolute owner of all things, we are tempted to use possessions selfishly by preventing others from using them even when we don't need them. That is, possessions can be used as power to rule other people.

The Christian response to God as owner is quite different. The use God has permitted us to have is based on a trust relationship and management responsibility. We are granted the privilege of using and enjoying the possessions which God provides. The power inherent in possessions also makes it possible for us to use them for the good of other people. By using possessions to help others, we honor God and acknowledge his continuing and absolute ownership.

Old Testament writers regularly reminded God's people of his ownership of the world and of their proper use of it. As Moses recalled the events at Sinai and afterwards, he challenged the people: "Behold, to the Lord your God belong heaven and the highest heavens, the earth and all that is in it" (Deut. 10:14). Continuing his exaltation of God, Moses taught the people that "He executes justice for the orphan and the widow, and shows His love for the alien by giving him food and clothing. So show your love for the alien, for you were aliens in the land of Egypt" (Deut. 10:18-19).

A regular theme in the psalms of praise was the acknowledgment of God's ownership of the world. "The earth is the

Lord's, and all it contains, The world, and those who dwell in it" (Ps. 24:1). "The heavens are Thine, the earth also is Thine" (Ps. 89:11). The Christian hymn, "We Give Thee But Thine Own," affirms God's ownership in a similar fashion:

> We give Thee but Thine own,
> Whate'er the gift may be;
> All that we have is Thine alone,
> A trust, O Lord, from Thee.
> —William W. How

Recognizing God's ownership of the world is important to Christian money management. It guides our motives for using the power inherent in money. It is easier to remember that God owns the oceans and the mountains than to remember that God owns the money and the things we purchase with the money we earn.

The investment of ourselves in earning money tends to create an emotional attachment which dulls our acknowledgment that money, too, belongs to God. We are tempted to justify our use of money based on our personal investment in earning it rather than on God's ownership. William Byron, president of Bread for the World Education Fund, wrote: "If private owners admit that they own nothing absolutely, and that everything they possess has been entrusted to them by the one Lord and Owner of it all, then a biblically-based humanism will temper our sinful tendencies to use, produce and distribute wealth as if it really belonged to us."[2]

Familiarity, the daily getting and spending, likewise promotes a false illusion of ownership. Faithful Christian money management requires that you daily "remember the Lord your God, for it is He who is giving you power to make wealth, that He may confirm His covenant" (Deut. 8:18).

Ownership by Identity: Made in God's Image

Of our children we hear someone say, "They sure look a lot like you." They are recognizing whose offspring they are, to whom they belong, and who is responsible for them. Similarly, God identifies us as his: "God said, 'Let us make man in Our image, according to Our likeness' " (Gen. 1:26). We are set apart from all other creation as being special, in the likeness of God, nonetheless a creation of God which signifies his ownership.

It may be quite disarming for some people to realize that every time a purchase is made, regardless of its value, they reveal their degree of acceptance of God's ownership. Since we were made in the image of God, we have a continuing responsibility to be his image. This is God's expectation of us. As children are the extension of their parents, we are an extension of God. All earning and use of money should logically be guided by this standard. The implications for Christian money management are profound. The way we live is greatly determined by our use of money. Our reputation, good or bad, is established by how nearly we reflect the image of God in our use of the resources which he provides.

We are God's managers, his image in all the world. Life and substance are to be held very lightly in our hands. When we try to grasp life or substance, then they are destroyed or lost and God's image is defamed. We are precious and unique in all of God's creation; the world is special; everything belongs to God.

Few, if any, identifying characteristics of persons are more significant than being created in the image of God. It is evident that humanity was meant to have a special dignity, that we were to be nearest to God. The psalmist reflected this idea when he wrote: "Thou hast made him [man] a little lower than God, And dost crown him with glory and majesty!" (8:5). Based on the history of his dealings with humanity, God relates everything he does to persons. People are God's first concern, the climax of all creation.

Ownership by identity establishes our purpose. Psalm 24:1 not only affirms that God owns the world, but that he owns "those who dwell in it." A person asks, "Who am I?" The answer is obvious: every person is a creation of God; we belong to God. The answer is equally obvious when a person asks, "What is my purpose in life?" The purpose of every person is to image God in the world. Representing God is job one for people. Gerhard von Rad, in his commentary on Genesis, notes that pagan kings of the Old Testament period sometimes erected a statue of themselves in newly conquered lands, especially if it was distant from their headquarters. By placing an image of themselves in the captured land, the inhabitants were constantly reminded of the new ownership.[3] As God's image (representatives) in the world, we provide a constant reminder that God is owner.

PRINCIPLE TWO: Persons are managers.

The Assignment: Persons in Charge

The management assignment is a universal one; it is applicable and workable in any social, economic, political, or geographical setting. To be a manager is not an option. Every person born into the world is a creation of God with the same general assignment; the assignment goes with being God's highest creation. Understanding this should make us sensitive to the worth and dignity of every person, not just Christians in the Western world.

God's relationship to persons is active, never passive. History bears witness to this fact. Humanity's response to God must likewise be an active response. Imaging God in the world requires action. But what kind of action? How can we image God? By conduct or disposition? By being "good"? Maybe by being pious, whatever that might mean. If imaging God requires action, is there some physical thing we can do?

Subdue and Rule Over

Created in the image of God, people are to reflect God in their relationship to, care for, and use of all of God's world. Everything we do reflects the kind of relationship we have with God. We can choose to image God in everything we do, especially the physical, down-to-earth kinds of things. What we are to do is described in the Bible as an assignment by God to man. "God blessed them; and God said to them, 'Be fruitful and multiply, and fill the earth, and subdue it; and rule over the fish of the sea and over the birds of the sky, and over every living thing that moves on the earth'" (Gen. 1:28).

God put people in charge of his world! The key words in the Scripture passage are *subdue* and *rule over*. They constitute a management assignment. (Since the word *stewardship* in the Bible means management, this is the beginning point for any doctrine of stewardship.) Animals live by instinct and basically cannot further God's creative work except to reproduce their own kind. But people can and are expected to do more than just reproduce. Someone has observed that of all the things God assigned people to do, being fruitful and multiplying and filling the earth is the only things they have done well.

When God created, he brought order out of chaos. But it is as though he did not completely banish chaos; he left something for us to do. It was yet to be subdued and brought under God's control; so he put people in charge with the awesome task of continuing his work of creation.

In our daily activities, it is usually a joy to be put in charge of something. To be put in charge boosts our morale and causes us to feel approval—trusted, worth something. This is true at any age.

I remember well the first time I was put in charge of something. I was reared on a farm where there were cattle and hogs and other barnyard animals. When I was about six or seven years old, a litter of pigs was born. In the litter was a "runt" (a runt pig is one that is born much smaller than the others). According to the law of nature, runt pigs usually don't survive simply because they don't have the energy to compete with siblings for food. However, with proper nourishment they have the potential for normal growth. So Dad put me in charge of feeding the runt pig with a bottle. The pig and I both fared well—until the pig grew up to be a hog and had to be sold. It was like selling my best friend.

My first experience of being put in charge of something is illustrative of the management assignment God gave to us. Our assigned task is to take care of God's world for him. It is to be done with tender care. We are to manage God's world as he would manage it, in his image. This is expressed in Scripture: "Then the Lord God took the man and put him into the garden of Eden to cultivate it and keep it" (Gen. 2:15). The idea here was to nourish and protect that which belongs to God. Man's responsible relationship to the animals is also indicated when they were brought to Adam to name them (Gen. 2:19-20).

Being in charge is one expression of the freedom God gave to persons. This freedom is the stage for humanity's greatest creativity and potential. It provides the environment for maximum development and the greatest good. I marvel at the way nonaggressive people often excel when given freedom or challenged to do so. This is a constant source of joy and blessing for those of us privileged to teach others. It is particularly rewarding to watch young people grow and excel.

When God assigned to man the management responsibility for his world, the door was opened for people's greatest glory or their greatest tragedy. Freedom provides for both options. When put in charge, some people become tyrants. They grasp and abuse the material world and lord it over other people. Intentionally or unintentionally, they misinterpret the freedom and authority they have been given.

At age eighteen I joined the air force. Four weeks into basic training I was transferred to technical school. Still in training with the rank of airman basic (no stripes), I was made barrack's chief. With this assignment, I was given red epaulets to wear along with the green ones everyone else wore. It is amazing what two pieces of red felt displayed on an airman basic's shoulders can do to a person. Judging from the resentment of others toward me, I must have been as "bad" as any drill sergeant you've every met. Being in charge brought out my worst attributes. At that point I did not know how to handle the power of being in charge.

Examples of the Management Assignment

The use of money and material things penetrates every facet of our lives. If we were looking for the one area where we are most likely to fail God and each other, the use of wealth would be it. Of all the management responsibilities we have, we are most vulnerable in the regular management of money and of the things which money can buy. Human history attests to this fact.

However, the opposite can also be true. Our management of money provides a way for us to express our deepest commitment to God, to our family, and to God's mission in the world. When we manage our money out of a commitment to God, we are seldom out of tune with our other management responsibilities—conservation, ecology, world hunger, illiteracy, and mission evangelism, to name a few.

Examples, good and bad, of God's management assignment are illustrated in the lives of Old Testament people. Abraham's comings and goings and seeking direction for his life show how responsible management depends on a sensitivity and commitment to God. Abraham mostly made good decisions for his life and the lives of the people he was leading because he let God teach him how to be in charge. (See Gen. 12—25.)

One example is found in Genesis 14. A confederacy of kings captured Sodom and Gomorrah and took all of the people and goods. Abraham's nephew Lot lived in Sodom. A fugitive escaped and reported the capture to Abraham. After leading his army in the pursuit and capture of the invaders, Abraham returned to the valley of Shaveh where he met Melchizedek. There, "the king of Sodom said to Abram, 'Give the people to me and take the goods for yourself' " (v. 21). Abraham had given Melchizedek a tenth of the booty he had captured (v. 20). This signified, by the customs of the day, that he was going to keep the remainder of the goods for himself. The king of Sodom also interpreted his actions in this way, so he made a plea that at least the people be returned.

Abraham's reply illustrates the depth of his management understanding. Abraham addressed the king of Sodom, "I have sworn to the Lord God Most High, possessor of heaven and earth, that I will not take a thread or a sandal thong or anything that is yours, lest you should say, 'I have made Abram rich' " (vv. 22-23). Recognizing God as owner of heaven and earth, Abraham did not grasp the material or the power over other people. Rather, he worshiped God and served others.

Abraham's son Isaac followed his example. (See Gen. 24—

28.) But his nephew Lot (Gen. 13; 19) and his grandson Jacob (Gen. 25—35) were exceptions. However, Joseph, Jacob's son, is a classic example of management. After being sold into slavery by his brothers (Gen. 37), Joseph became a steward (manager) in Potiphar's house (Gen. 39:5). Later, as second in command to the king of Egypt, Joseph was the king's manager. He was fully authorized to represent the king and deal independently on his behalf (manage that which belonged to someone else). After his management success for the king of Egypt, Joseph had his own steward who managed his household (Gen. 43.16). As with Abraham, Joseph's management excellence was paralleled by an abiding commitment to honor God (Gen. 39:9).

Examples of God's management assignment are also expressed in the law of Moses as it applied to the way the people lived in faith and community. Every seventh year the land was to be left uncultivated that it might rebuild itself (Lev. 25:45). The year of Jubilee, the fiftieth year, included a provision for returning the land to its original owners (Lev. 25:10, 13). This was a management arrangement which kept the rich from getting richer at the expense of the poor. The good of both humanity and the earth are at the heart of God's management plan. This is true, for instance, when the Law directs that some of the harvest be left in the corners of the fields for aliens, orphans, and widows. (See Deut. 24:19-22.)

God's faithful people, as illustrated in the Old Testament, understood and accepted God as Creator and Owner of the heavens and the earth and all they contained. The thrust of all of God's dealings with his people anticipates a management response from them. When they chose to rebel against God, they expressed their rebellion by mismanagement. Many of the prophetic discourses rebuke the mismanagement by the people. From Isaiah's (1:16-17) and Amos's pleas for justice for the disenfranchised people to Malachi's charge that the people had departed from their God—all demonstrate a management problem.

God put us in charge of his world. Knowing ourselves as we do, we may not think that God was very smart to turn over such a mammoth management task to us. But I can't think of a better arrangement I would want to be involved in. Whatever God assigns us to do which pleases him will be the very best thing we can do.

Notes

1. I have dealt briefly with the material contained in chapters 1 and 2 in another book I coauthored: Lee E. Davis and Ernest D. Standerfer, *Christian Stewardship in Action* (Nashville: Convention Press, 1983), pp. 30-37.

2. William J. Byron, "The Ethics of Stewardship," *The Earth Is the Lord's: Essays on Stewardship*, eds. Mary Evelyn Jegen and Bruno Manno (New York: Paulist Press, 1978), p. 49.

3. Gerhard von Rad, *Genesis: A Commentary*, trans. John H. Marks (Philadelphia: Westminster Press, 1961), pp. 57-58.

2
Christians in Charge and Responsible

Illustrations from the Old Testament have shown that management is the expected, natural response of people to God. Thus it should be no surprise to find that *the principle that man is a manager* of God's world is continued and given expanded meaning in the New Testament. There is a notable difference: the responsibility is greater.

Management as Taught in the New Testament

Studying the Old Testament can be most helpful in understanding and applying the teachings of the New Testament. This is especially true in understanding how Christians continue to be in charge.

Building on Old Testament Teachings

The uniqueness and purpose of each person are established by being created in the image of God (Gen. 1:26). For people to have freedom to fulfill this unique role and purpose, God put us in charge of the world. The assignment was to subdue and rule over creation (Gen. 1:28). But man failed to live up to his uniqueness, and thus he failed to fulfill his purpose; he sinned against God. (We live with the impact of that failure and our own failure daily.)

When man chose to sever his relationship with God by sinning, God took the initiative to reestablish it. "The man and his wife hid themselves from the presence of the Lord God. . . . Then the Lord God called to the man, and said to him, 'Where are you?' " (Gen. 3:8-9). Much of the rest of the Bible is a record of how God sought to restore to persons the glory he gave in creation.

The climax of God's initiative to redeem us was the gift of his Son, Jesus Christ. "God so loved the world, that He gave His only begotten Son" (John 3:16). The possibility of a new level of relating to God was ushered in by Christ. God's love for us was never absent, but never was it more evident than in Christ. The image of God in man was not canceled by sin, but it was unrecognizably marred. Christ revealed God's love for us and provided a human example of a person's potential when reconciled to God. As Christians, God's love for us and our love for God and other people explain why our management for God is even deeper than a general assignment for all people.

The New Testament builds on the Old Testament teaching of man in God's image. Paul wrote that man "is the image and glory of God" (1 Cor. 11:7); and James wrote that people "have been made in the likeness of God" (Jas. 3:9). These references seem like quotes from the Old Testament. But here is the effective difference: the meaning is redirected to Christ as the perfect reflection of God: "He [Christ] is the radiance of His [God's] glory and the exact representation of His nature" (Heb. 1:3). It was and is God's plan in sending Christ into the world that we should "be conformed to the image of his Son" (Rom. 8:29). In Christ the image of God given us in creation is seen most clearly.

Management in Christ's Teachings

In the Old Testament, the image of God in man was to be expressed by subduing and ruling over creation as God would do it himself. I have interpreted this as a management assignment which anticipates a management response. But the creation account does not use the word *management;* it simply describes the activity. If there should be any lingering doubt about the appropriateness of this interpretation, the words used in the New Testament should dispel it. (In understanding Christian management, the word study approach is indispensable.)

To describe a similar but more comprehensive activity than subduing and ruling over, Jesus and the New Testament writers used a word which means manager. It is the Greek word *oikonomos.* This is a compound word. The first root is *oikos.* It is a noun which means "house." The second root, *nomos,* is a noun for "law." Together as a compound word, *oikonomos* literally means "the law of the house" which contains a management idea.

In the Greek culture within which Jesus' teachings were written, an *oikonomos* was the chief servant in a household; he administered the law of the house. He was sometimes the most trusted slave or could be a freeman. (English translations of the New Testament usually translate *oikonomos* as "steward.") As it is used in the New Testament, *oikonomos* means primarily "manager of something that belongs to someone else." When you read "steward" in the Bible, that's what it means.

Of Jesus' parables which use *oikonomos,* Luke 12:41-48 is a good example. This parable is often referred to as the parable of the faithful and unfaithful steward.

> And Peter said, "Lord, are You addressing this parable to us, or to everyone else as well?" And the Lord said, "Who then is the faithful and sensible steward, whom his master will put in charge of his servants, to give them their rations at the proper time? Blessed is that slave whom his master finds so doing when he comes. Truly I say to you, that he will put him in charge of all his possessions. But if that slave says

in his heart, 'My master will be a long time in coming,' and begins to beat the slaves, both men and women, and to eat and drink and get drunk; the master of that slave will come on a day when he does not expect him, and at an hour he does not know, and will cut him in pieces, and assign him a place with the unbelievers. And that slave who knew his master's will and did not get ready or act in accord with his will, shall receive many lashes, but the one who did not know it, and committed deeds worthy of a flogging, will receive but few. And from everyone who has been given much shall much be required; and to whom they entrusted much, of him they will ask all the more."

Luke introduced the parable with a question from Peter to Jesus about a preceding parable (v. 41). In that parable Jesus taught his listeners to "be like men who are waiting for their master when he returns from the wedding feast" (v. 36). Peter wanted to know to whom Jesus was addressing the parable, just to the disciples or to everyone? Jesus answered with the parable quoted here which indicates it is for all.

In verse 42, steward (*oikonomos*) is a person. Verses 43 to 48 describe the steward's (manager's) activity. As noted earlier, where a management situation exists, three relationships are involved. It is true in this parable: the owner relates to his property, the owner and manager relate to each other, and the manager relates to the owner's property. The parable suggests a present life situation based on our understanding of Christ's mission in the world: the owner is God; the manager is humanity, and the property is everything God has entrusted to us—life, powers, influence, and resources. In the context of the New Testament, people are responsible and accountable to God for the effective management of every element as a means of continuing Christ's mission.

The significant difference in understanding Old and New Testament management is Christ's birth. People were managers accountable to God before Christ but were not understood on such a personal level. The purpose for Christian management has been greatly enlarged. As managers for God through Christ, we are to care as he cares for all of his creation. Since we live in community with others, we must also relate to and care for fellow humanity. Everything that God does relates to people. To image God in our management includes an active use of our abilities to care for other people as God cares for them. Christian management is redemptive activity.

As you would expect, the fullest understanding of God's management assignment is found in the gospel of Christ. Christ as the perfect image of God (John 1:18; Heb. 1:3) provides the reference point. As the perfect manager, Christ made God and his management assignment completely understandable and attainable. As our perfect example, Christ reaffirmed the boundless possibilities of a human life when reconciled to God. With the freedom and creativity God gave to people, the potential for creative management of life and resources is almost without limit.

Management in the New Testament simply cannot be understood apart from Christ's mission. Relating the two gives me hope and optimism for the future. The plans God placed in motion for our creative relationship with him in Christ are breathtaking. As with man in creation, Christians have an up-front, hands-on, personal stake in what God is doing. The stage was perfectly set for the mission Christ gave to Christians individually and together as the church.

You and I are benefactors of that mission as well as participants. As participants, we have a personal management responsibility for Christ's continuing mission to man. One sure measure of our acceptable participation is the quality of our management, especially money management.

Responsible Management and Christ's Mission

Since beginning a personal plan of money management, I've realized that I was not a very effective Christian before. My thoughts, energies, and resources were mostly consumed on myself and my family.

The patience God has! For some twenty years of my adult Christian life, I basically understood Christ's mission but had little freedom to respond with material resources to new opportunities of service. Lack of money kept me from doing a lot of good things I could have done. I thought it was because of a low salary—a sacrifice I was having to make. Such rationalization may help us survive during our most depressed periods, but it finally creates resentment.

It created resentment for me. When I was a pastor, I recall inviting a missionary to speak during the annual mission emphasis. At the end of the worship service, he challenged each family to give the equivalent of one week's salary for the special foreign mission offering that year. That was fine for others, but I could rationalize that my family couldn't afford to give that much because of our "circumstances." But then he had the audacity to ask everyone who would make that commitment to come forward. I was pastor; what could I do? I had to be the example. I resented it.

Was the missionary wrong in his challenge? Is it wrong for Christians to be challenged to be more than they are? Are Christians' personal money management and Christ's mission related? Does success in the mission of the church depend on the effectiveness of Christians' personal money management? You may resent me for raising these questions!

To see how our personal management relates to Christ's mission, consider first the nature of the mission assignment.

The Mission Assignment as Management

In essence, the mission assignment God gave to Christians is this: "Do what I've been doing since creation—bring order out of chaos." But because Christ has come, our actions are to be related to him. Humanity's first assignment was similar but more general. It was to serve God by continuing the creative process, increasing order by reducing chaos. Accomplishing the assignment required the forethought inherent in management, of being in charge of God's world.

The mission assignment in the New Testament added depth and gave more specific direction to God's initial assignment. The circumstances had changed; man had sinned; he had reintroduced chaos. Thus a specific assignment was necessary. As was true in creation, God gave people priority in the new assignment. People's at oneness with God—reconciliation, redemption, recreation—became the primary objective in God's "eternal purpose which He carried out in Christ Jesus our Lord" (Eph. 3:11).

In two ways, Paul illustrated how our management is a continuation of God's own actions and how it unquestionably establishes Christians as managers for God. In the first instance, Paul refers to God's redemptive activity as management. "In all wisdom and insight He made known to us the mystery of His will, . . . with a view to an administration [*oikonomia,* management] suitable to the fulness of the times, that is, the summing up of all things in Christ, things in the heavens and things upon the earth" (Eph. 1:8-10). (In the King James Version, *oikonomia* is translated "dispensation" in verse 10.) Paul's understanding of what God had been doing in the world and for people from the beginning of time was management. Sending Christ as man's Savior was a climatic expression of God's management.

Admittedly, there is a problem when the concept of God

as a manager is pressed too far. It breaks down when the definition of manager is applied to the management of something that belongs to someone else. This suggests a responsibility to another, a time of accounting for one's actions. This can be resolved, however, when the thrust of all that is revealed of God's nature in the Bible is considered. God is responsible to himself, to his nature. He will not violate his nature or his purpose, thus the accounting for his management actions were to his nature and purpose previously established. More important, however, is how our management is intimately connected to God's management, how we have a mission which is a continuation of God's mission.

Paul provides the understanding: "If indeed you have heard of the stewardship [*oikonomia*] of God's grace which was given to me for you; that by revelation there was made known to me the mystery" (Eph. 3:2-3). The mystery which God made known to Paul was that the Gentiles were to be included in recreation made possible in Christ. Since the Jewish people were the first object of God's redemptive activity, the inclusion of the Gentiles meant that Christ's mission was to all people of the world.

For the purpose of revealing this, Paul wrote, "I was made a minister, according to the gift of God's grace . . . to bring to light what is the administration [*oikonomia*] of the mystery which for ages has been hidden in God, who created all things; in order that the manifold wisdom of God might now be made known through the church" (Eph. 3:7-9). (See also Col. 1:25-27.) God's management is a plan to redeem Jews and Gentiles. Christians can begin to understand the purpose for their management as they understand more fully the purpose of God's management. When this is understood, what becomes evident is that God's management is an example for Christians' management.

Why was Paul so "fired up" about sharing Christ with the Gentiles? Why was he willing to let himself be stoned by nonbelieving Jews and imprisoned in his efforts to share Christ? Why did he travel all over Asia, often at great risk to his life, to preach and establish churches? Why would he work at tentmaking to earn money to help support his work?

Paul understood God's assignment and Christ's commission to be personal. What is our personal stake in sharing Christ's gospel with the world? "Go therefore and make disciples of all the nations" (Matt. 28:19). "As the Father has sent Me, I also send you" (John 20:21). "You shall be My witnesses both in Jerusalem, and in all Judea and Samaria, and even to the remotest part of the earth" (Acts 1:8). Are these instructions personal for all Christians or are they the responsibility of some vague group of people commonly known as "they," church people in general?

The Mission Assignment and the Church

What do football fans do that causes you to know they like football? They support their home team. That may mean financial support, but more important it means personal involvement. In God's management for the ages, he seeks a personal relationship with each person through Christ. Within that saving relationship, each Christian is responsible for helping accomplish Christ's mission in the world; each one is accountable to God for his or her level of involvement.

As a way of supporting their team, football fans may organize into a fan club. This gives unity of purpose to their support; it strengthens their support of the team. The church is certainly more than a fan club because it has a divine origin, but individual Christians are made stronger for their task when involved with a local church. In fact, Christ assigned his continuing mission to the church.

After Peter's confession at Caesarea Philippi that Christ was the Son of the living God, Christ said, "Upon this rock I will build My church; and the gates of Hades shall not overpower it. I will give you the keys of the kingdom of heaven" (Matt. 16:18-19). With this the church was founded and the mission assigned; Christ's mission became the mission of the church. Since Christ's mission was assigned to the church, a Christian cannot understand what he is to do without first understanding the mission of the church.

This was what Paul was referring to in Ephesians 3:9. The mystery that salvation through Christ was for all people was to be made known through the church. As in a fan club, there is strength in unity. Within the fellowship of the church, the multiple gifts of each member can be directed to the various ministries which make up the whole mission. This concept is supported by the overarching management plan of God which has been at work since creation. Each person is created with unique abilities which are to be managed so as to contribute most to the accomplishment of God's total mission expressed fully in Christ. Mission support is personal, but it is more effective when combined with the support of other Christians through the church.

I've used the word *mission* and the word *ministries*. They are not the same. Ministries are the various tasks necessary to accomplish the mission. It helps me to think in terms of one mission. The only mission is God's which was given to the church through Christ. Thus the mission of the church is accomplished by Christians as they minister in different ways. The many tasks equal the various ministries necessary to accomplish the one mission. I use the terms *mission support, mission work,* and *mission ministries* to magnify the one mission and to avoid the possibility of ever identifying any one ministry as the mission, as an end in itself.

There is one mission; there is a biblical precedent for serving Christ within the fellowship of the church. Where does management, particularly money management, fit into the plan?

It may help to reflect upon Peter's question to Jesus in the parable again: "Lord, are You addressing this parable to us, or to everyone else as well" (Luke 12:41). Jesus answered Peter with a parable which described the actions of an individual manager. The accountability which Christ expects is obviously personal. The next question is how? How can we Christians express our responsibility for Christ's mission to the world?

Mission Support

Living life as a manager is God's design for every person. For Christians, management suggests being in control and being disciplined. It suggests having goals and a plan of action. It requires sensitivity to all the events and people surrounding a person's life. Maturing, growing, adapting, evaluating, and choosing priorities are expected. All of these factors and more characterize a Christian's mission support. This is idealism. It may become vague, intangible, up there somewhere unless we choose to bring it down to earth.

Christ was the great idealist, but an idealist who gave tangible expression to his ideals. He understood God's design for management dating back to creation. From the beginning, God's management assignment to the human race was focused in management of the material world. Pleasing God meant managing properly the material things God had let surround each person. That has not changed. Mission support is much more than money, as just indicated, but all of the other support factors will be diminished or absent when a Christian does not practice money management.

Referring again to Jesus' parable in Luke 12, *oikonomos* (v. 42) is a noun translated "steward" or "manager." As noted, verses 43 through 48 describe the manager's activities related to the household. These activities include distribution of food and supplies necessary to the livelihood of the others in the household and for the completion of the tasks assigned to them by their master. Luke 16:2 uses the word *oikonomein* to express this distributing activity: "Give an account of your stewardship, for you can no longer be steward" (*oikonomein*, do the distributing).

Thus an important element of a Christian's management is distribution. As Christians, distributing (using, giving) that which God lets surround us is for the purpose of fulfilling the mission assignment God has given through Christ.

All things considered, one of the most visible expressions of a contemporary Christian's mission support is giving money. One might argue that giving money without giving self is vain giving. I also know what Jesus taught: "Where your treasure is, there will your heart be also" (Matt. 6:21). In more familiar language, where your investments are, that's where your interests will be. We may as well face the facts; as with all our ancestors, one of our great sins is selfishness expressed as mismanagement. We choose more often to use our money for ourselves than for support of Christ's mission. The result is that we are more interested in ourselves.

I continue to struggle with hindrances to giving though I can see much growth since coming to understand God's management principles more fully. But the struggle is to be expected; my old nature resists my new nature. The new nature says manage my money for God. The old nature says manage it for myself. It has been so since the fall of humanity.

If I tried to rank my hindrances to giving, materialism would probably be first on the list. For many years, materialism determined how I lived my life; it taught me that money was very important, and it caused me to develop a craving for material things. The end result was mismanagement because I used my money unwisely.

Second, excessive dependence upon credit created a financial merry-go-round from which I couldn't dismount. One bad management decision fostered another. Giving through my church was a burden; I couldn't afford to give generously, and what I did give was seldom cheerfully given. My reasoning told me I was poor because I had no surplus money. Where each paycheck would be spent was decided long before I received it because of payments for credit.

Addiction to material things and the use of credit create a near universal hindrance to Christian giving in the Western world. But there is a third hindrance to giving which also appears to have a near universal dimension. It is ignorance. For many years I did not know what the Bible taught about management.

Before I understood the biblical principle of management, my giving could be described as giving by the law and giving out of duty. Let's analyze my previous giving motives in light of Christian management. First, look at law. Is it possible to legislate mission support?

We are so accustomed to laws that it would be difficult to function in life without them. We refer to the laws of the universe, international law, civil laws, traffic laws, and other laws when trying to justify our position or point of view. After all, we reason, how could the world be civilized without laws? Knowing our own tendencies to stray because of poor discipline obviously proves the need for the restraints of law. Certainly Christ did not teach that every Christian could do what seemed right in his own eyes without regard to others or God. It is true, however, that if every person in the world reflected the image of Christ, there would be no need for enforced laws.

To live or give only by law distorts our uniqueness which God gave us in creation. Where law is or must be strictly enforced, people under that law are made to respond with a sameness. Law limits the freedom of a person's individual, unique response to life's circumstances. The restraints of law tend to reduce the natural expressions of the higher spiritual life.

When applying law to Christian giving, it should be done ever so carefully. One requirement of Christian management is giving; a nongiving Christian is a contradiction of terms. Christians are best known by their giving. So in essence, there is a Christian law for giving. But Jesus was careful in this. I know of no occasion where he motivated giving by a law. The thrust of his teachings on giving is always beyond law. "Freely you received, freely give" (Matt. 10:8). His illustrations and commendations point to those such as the widow who gave her coins and received Jesus' highest praise (Mark 12:41-44), and Mary who lavishly anointed him with expensive perfume (Luke 7:37-38). Jesus encouraged giving which was motivated by inner commitment and love for God.

Then there is duty. Duty consciousness is a commendable characteristic. Duty is usually based on a sense of what is right and fair. Others receive consideration as the duty-conscious person finds his place in the flow of life. There is more freedom in duty than in law.

But there is a built-in flaw in the duty motive. It is based on conscience, and conscience is fallible. Conscience is influenced by social standards and expectations which can be more secular than Christian. Conscience differs from person to person depending on that person's environment, and it often fluctuates with social relationships as well as physical and mental orientation. There is a place in Christian commitment and giving for duty, however. Belonging to God and a fellowship of Christians anticipates duty consciousness.

But consider why it is risky to base mission support on law and a sense of duty. Giving based on law or a sense of duty may cause you to give today, but you may have to be convinced again tomorrow. If you are confronted with repetitious appeals for law and/or duty giving, you tend to ignore them unless the appeals become increasingly more demanding. Reduced giving and the necessity of stronger appeals simply increase your level of frustration and diminish your growth as a Christian. Resentment is likely to follow.

Giving as a natural part of Christian management is altogether positive. It emphasizes the freedom God gave to people in creation. It places the emphasis on the growth of the giver instead of the gift, which is what all of God's relationships to us do. It challenges us to be the image of God, "imitators of God, as beloved children" (Eph. 5:1). It increases our responsibility, but it likewise increases our joy and contentment. In responsible freedom, we give what God wants us to give to accomplish his mission assignment.

Giving out of freedom is prompted by love for God. A commitment to manage your life, powers, influence, and resources expresses your love for God, other people, and the material world. When you give because of your commitment to Christian management, you will not have to be convinced again the next week or month. The church is not just another organization trying to separate you from your money. It is a unified fellowship of Christians on mission in the world. Giving is the way of Christian living; it is confession, worship, and service—participation in God's recreative mission.

Truly, Christians are in charge and are responsible. The likelihood of fulfilling the assigned mission without Christian commitment to a management life-style is minimal. But there is reason for hope; God trusted us, so we should trust ourselves. Think of it this way. When God first created people and put us in charge, he had already made all of the necessary physical arrangements for human success.

That's the situation now. God has already provided enough material resources for us to provide for our families, live as responsible citizens in society, and support his mission assignment. Mission support is not in competition with the other two. Commitment to and the practice of Christian money management will clearly demonstrate this fact.

Part
2
Shaping a Christian Life-Style

3
Life-style Contrasts: Secular and Christian

Contrasts exist in people and nature. Many of the contrasts are pleasing; "Variety is the spice of life," it has been said. But all spice in life may not be worth the price that must be paid to have it. Secular life-style is an example. To choose a secular life-style is to organize life as though there is no God or as though God doesn't count. Materialism is the nucleus, and material things become as important or more important than people. People are reduced to objects. Life is viewed as economic development. The price one pays for a secular life is insecurity, frustration, and lack of contentment and hope. Notable in the list is lack of hope. A secular life-style may result in the accumulation of many things, but it doesn't provide for hope after death.

A Christian life-style in contrast is a particular, unique way of living as taught and illustrated by Christ. It is an intentional way of living; it is purposeful, thought-out, consciously chosen, and Christ-centered. A Christian life-style is one that needs minimum reshaping. People are of ultimate importance. Material things are good but only a means of living and serving.

A deacon friend and mentor of mine in the first church where I was a pastor illustrated the contrasting outcomes of secular and Christian life-styles. We were working together on the church grounds. I noticed that he had stopped the tractor and was just sitting still in deep thought. Like an inquisitive child, I interrupted him. "Is something wrong?"

Without irritation he responded, "I'm thinking about what we're doing." Such a purposeful, thought-out, consciously chosen approach to work characterized his whole life. Then he explained his actions. "Pastor, most people I know who get into trouble do so because they don't think about what they're doing—what the outcome of their actions will be. Because they don't think ahead, they waste a lot of time redoing and undoing what they did wrong."

My deacon friend exemplified the Christian approach to life; his analysis of people who don't consider the outcome of their actions typifies a secular life. The contrast is especially evident in the outcome. At the conclusion of life, management decisions and actions appear to be one basis for Christ's judgment. Someone has said, "We are what we are because of what we've been. And we are fast becoming what we will always be." We need to consciously face the choice of what we are and what we are becoming. It is important to know that we have two options.

Life-styles are shaped by many forces. Customs passed from one generation to another often mold our life-styles. Environment also influences them. Christian faith or the lack of it definitely shapes our style of living. Frequently, however, it's not a conscious choice based on any particular value system. It simply evolves as a way of living influenced by the trends of contemporary culture. Secular influences on our life-styles can be very subtle; changes can be made unconsciously. This will be evident in the following discussion on contemporary life-styles.

PRINCIPLE THREE: **The biblical doctrine of management shapes a Christian's life-style.**

Contemporary Life-styles

Columbus, the famed discoverer, is reported to have said: "He who possesses gold does all that he wishes in this world, and succeeds in helping souls into paradise."[1] History and the way many of us now live have proven that many Christians with gold do all they wish in the world more often than helping non-Christians know Christ. If our present direction continues, T. S. Eliot's sarcastic prophecy may well come true. He supposedly concluded that when our civilization has perished,

> The wind shall say, "Here were decent
> godless people,
> Their only monument the asphalt road,
> And a thousand lost golf balls."[2]

Life-style Conceived in Secularism

The term *life-style* is of recent origin. The 1961 editions of Webster's and Funk and Wagnalls's dictionaries do not list the word *life-style*. However, psychologist Alfred Adler [1870-1937] did introduce the term in psychological studies much earlier.[3] In the more recent introduction of the term, it was conceived in a thoroughly secular environment.

In 1970 a book by Charles Reich was published with the title *The Greening of America.* In this book, Reich provides a commentary on secular life-style which evolved in the 1960s. To distinguish this new generation from previous ones, he identifies three general types of consciousness. "One was formed in the nineteenth century, the second in the first half of this century, the third is just emerging [that is, in the late 1960s]. Consciousness I is the traditional outlook of the American farmer, small businessman, and worker who is trying to get ahead. Consciousness II represents the values of an organized society. Consciousness III is the new generation."[4]

Reich uses the term *consciousness* as "a total configuration in any given individual, which makes up his whole perception of reality, his whole world view."[5] The new generation popularized the word *life-style* and contrasted their life-style choices to the previous generations with the concept of "alternate" life-styles—moral freedom, open marriages, swinging singles, and such.

Times were prosperous in the 1960s. Credit was easy for the consumer to get and apparently profitable to the lender. Depression-conditioned parents were reading John Kenneth Galbraith's *The Affluent Society*. They were giving their children all of the things their parents couldn't provide for them when they were children. And in the 1960s there were a lot of children in their late teens and early twenties, children of the postwar baby boom. Striving to grow up and establish their own identities, many of these young people rejected their parents' values, especially material values. These older teens and young adults were prime candidates for alternate life-styles. Thus the "hippies," demonstrators, drug culture, and other groups became more visible.

With time, many of the alternate life-style patterns were culturally accommodated. Fashion was one thing; median and even some senior adults copied the younger generation by growing beards, letting their hair grow longer, and dressing more casually. When parents began to look like their children, rejecting their parents' materialistic values no longer served a purpose. In the evolution the young adults generally reverted to their parents' materialistic values.

But the pattern of undisciplined living had been established. Much had been lost; sexual morality in particular had been severely eroded. Then a similar thing happened with morality generally as with fashion; the more open, vulgar style of life attained cultural acceptance. Granted, there have always been those who choose alternate life-styles and live immorally. But immorality had now reached a new high, or low. Anyway, there was more of it.

The market place capitalized on every aspect of the evolving cultural demands. That should be no surprise. We seem to eventually relate everything to economics. From history we learn that at one time the church was selling pieces of wood which reportedly came from Christ's cross to raise money for the church. Entertainment and commerce gladly accommodated consumers' growing appetites for more things and more of the erotic. Mass media, through entertainment and advertising, became a most influential force in determining material and moral values. More than ever before, the media used the science of behavior modification.

Products of a Secular Life-style

Theologically, one of the most demeaning characteristics of the emerging new life-style was reducing persons to objects (dehumanization), a commodity to be marketed. The increased acceptance of materialistic values and the decrease in moral and spiritual values created the proper climate. As a part of secularism (organizing life as though there is no God), materialism measures the worth of everything including people by sales and consumption. John Kavanaugh, associate professor of philosophy at Saint Louis University, has called this the commodity ethic.[6] All things are motivated by profit. Our worth is measured by our ability to consume, to increase profits.

The human body as an object is itself plundered for profit.

Advertising creates an image of inadequacy. We are portrayed as marred, scarred, stretched, and aged (heaven forbid). Not only that, our breath and body odors are so offensive not even our family and best friends would risk telling us. The cure, of course, is to buy the right product. It's easy to be loved if you use a certain cologne. There's a "de-aging expert" on the market too, a seventh day scrub cream. And don't forget to thank your mouthwash!

Western people generally are obsessed with being gratified, a literal addiction to material things and pleasure. Exploitations of these base desires are so obvious that it seems hardly necessary to mention them. Ad people have made us believe that we deserve all we can get. Even if it costs more, "we're worth it." And owning one kind of automobile promises to save and set you free.

The new life-style has struck its most devastating blow in the area of relationships. Reducing people to craving objects makes caring relationships impossible. When portrayed as objects, people relate to each other as objects. Personal relationships such as those between spouses, parents and children, and friends lose much of their value. Relationships between objects require no emotional involvement, commitment, or responsibility. These are qualities reserved for human relationships. Such cherished relationships are replaced with objects which can be bought. "I bought a wagon (auto) out of wedlock . . . it looked like it . . . needed me." "This baby (auto) won't keep you up nights." "How to cradle your twelve-year-old (Scotch)." "Think of her (an airline stewardess) as your mother." It seems that human relationships are expected to wear out much like one's washing machine. In fact, many marriages are not lasting much longer on the average than washing machines.

The glamor and glory portrayed in much of the advertising is designed to make us discontent with what we are and what we have. Relationships between spouses are influenced by this manufactured discontentment. It causes us to have unreasonable, maybe impossible, expectations of our mates. This is especially true in size, proportions, weight, and adornment. Such dissatisfaction was illustrated in a recent television poll in my city. The question was asked, "If you had it to do over, would you choose the same mate?" Thirty-six percent of the respondents answered "no."[7] And they were still living together!

Relationships, particularly family ones, have taken on the cultural characteristics of merchandising—fast-food restaurants and disposable containers, for instance. At the least slowdown, we change or throw it away and get another one (relationship). Consumerism is antifamily for profit's sake. Kavanaugh, as well as others, notes that the stronger the family relationships the greater the resistance to dehumanization.[8] When people are relating to others as people rather than as objects, there is more contentment and less buying to satisfy feelings of inadequacy. No wonder the family is being assaulted more than ever. In dollars, it's profitable.

The sixties come-of-age generation made intentional life-style choices in rebelling against their parents' material values. But because the choices were made in a spiritual vacuum, the degeneration of other values which followed were received as casual by-products, although unintentional. That has certainly been the trend among all ages since then. The personal intimacy which wouldn't have been tolerated in the theater twenty-five years ago is now being viewed in our homes on primetime television.

Our life-styles have been tested at three crucial points: spiritual, moral, and material. Because we lacked the first, we failed in the other two. What has developed is the very opposite of a Christian life-style; we have chosen to live life unmanaged, undisciplined, purposeless, not thought out, unintentional. Remember what my deacon friend said: "Most people I know who get into trouble do so because they don't think about what they're doing—what the outcome of their actions will be." That's prophetic when applied to our evolving life-styles. One of the best measures of the inadequacy of our chosen life-style is the evident and continuing lack of contentment among Christians and non-Christians alike. As the deacon said, when we don't think ahead we waste a lot of time redoing and undoing what we did wrong.

After this brief survey of secular life-style, consider the contrasting Christian life-style.

Christian Life-style

A Christian life-style is shaped by intentionally choosing to embrace biblical principles and values. It's expressed as "the habitual ways in which an individual works, eats, drinks, recreates, worships, entertains himself, and relates to others."[9] It's more than one's standard of living, which is a kind of summary statement for the various aspects of life-style just mentioned. Standard of living refers specifically to the quantity and quality of material things used in everyday life.[10]

Life-style is the pattern that emerges in all that an individual does in his daily routine. Christian life-style is an organized way of life with one's commitment to Christ at the center of life. It affirms what Paul wrote: "By Him all things were created, both in the heavens and on earth, visible and invisible, whether thrones or dominions or rulers or authorities—all things have been created by Him and for Him. And He is before all things, and in Him all things hold together" (Col. 1:16-17).

I don't know of a better place to learn about Christian life-style than Jesus' Sermon on the Mount. Here's expert advice on how to live life. I've chosen passages cafeteria-style from the sermon to illustrate its life-style applications, but there's hardly a verse that doesn't apply.

The Unique Quality of Christian Life-style

Christian life-style has a quality of *simplicity:* "Blessed are the pure in heart, for they shall see God" (Matt. 5:8). When I read some passages of Scripture, I automatically translate them into mental images. This one used to translate "grand-mother." Grandmother was an old, godly woman. I supposed that she was about the purest in heart as anyone could get. So my interpretation of Matthew 5:8 was this: Christians like Grandmother will be the ones who get to see God. "Pure in heart" addresses the simplification of life.

Gerald Mann, a Baptist pastor in Texas, quotes Thoreau as writing, "In proportion as I have simplified my existence, I have found the universe to be friendly; in proportion as I have complexified my existence, I have found the universe to be hostile."[11] Grandmother was a simple, godly woman. As best as I could tell, she had one God and a simple faith in him. The verse says people with single allegiance to God will get to see him.

Contrasted with contemporary life-styles, there is a great gulf which separates the two. The words I hear most often to describe life-style are "hectic" or "run to death." Single allegiance is difficult when we are involved at the office, the club, board of directors meetings, with investment management, in political meetings, PTA, sports, house-cars-boat upkeep, the family, and one day and three nights per week at church. This kind of life-style is typical of many Christians. Idolatry is having more than one God. The duplicity of secular, consumer oriented life-styles elaborated earlier provides an even greater contrast.

Jesus also used the word *blessed* in the verse, which translates "happy." Happiness is often identified with feelings. David Beckmann, a World Bank economist, identifies three feelings associated with happiness.[12] The first is a temporary feeling we get when we meet or exceed our expectations. This is a moment-by-moment measure of one's sense of welfare. The second is contentment, which depends on inner spiritual resources. It's a lack of anxiety about tomorrow and all of the future. Finally, happiness is defined by a satisfied feeling with one's lot in life. This person may be anxious and live a hectic life, simply unaware that there is another option. Thus he's happy with what he has.

In the context of the verse, Jesus used "happy" in the sense of inner spiritual resources. Happy are those people who have one goal in life: to live a Christian life-style. After faith in Christ, management is the necessary approach to simplify your life. Disorganized, unintentional living produces equal amounts of frustration and unhappiness. Money management is logical; it provides an organized base of operation for the individual or family. After my family made a commitment to Christian money management, one of the first apparent benefits was feeling that life was more simple. According to Jesus, a person's degree of happiness is directly related to the degree of life-style simplicity. And simplicity begins to happen when life is organized around God.

Another unique quality of Christian life-style is *preserving* (being like salt) and *pointing* (being like light). To all disciples Jesus taught: "You are the salt of the earth. . . . You are the light of the world" (Matt. 5:13-14). In other words you are to be a part of the solution, not a part of the problem. Overriding concerns in our nation change as reflected in the news headlines each day. But whether it's unrest in the Middle East or South America, unemployment, inflation, a nuclear power plant crisis, or something else, everything is related to economics. The number one national problem is economics reflected in the federal deficit.

Applying what Jesus taught here, what should Christians be doing to preserve a stable society? As with an individual's or a family's budget, a deficit occurs in the federal budget when more money is spent than is received. A great amount of the federal money congress authorizes to be spent is for programs which directly benefit all of us. Many of the decisions to spend are prompted by our insistence. Wanting to be reelected, members of congress honor as many demands as possible. This has happened for so long that we have become government dependent. Many have come to believe that we deserve to be taken care of by our government. Not only do we demand necessities but comfort. We have become a nation spoiled by a government insured life-style of comfort. As a whole, Christians do not act much differently than non-Christians in their demands. We are not functioning as preservers in the matter of economics.

Our national situation reminds me of an experience my friend Mr. Johnston had with his goat. He bought a billy goat to eat briars and vines on a vacant lot next to his. (Goats will eat just about anything they can chew, and maybe some they can't chew.) By staking the goat on a long rope, it had served its purpose well. Then a friend asked Mr. Johnston about borrowing his billy goat for a different purpose. Mr. Johnston agreed. Several months passed before it was returned.

When he put the goat back in the vacant lot, it just stood around bleatting; it wouldn't attempt to eat the briars and vines. Mr. Johnston called his friend to find out what had happened to his goat. He discovered that it had been living in luxury while on loan—bought feed, petting, the works. Its natural instincts to eat rough food and live out in the open had been replaced by a life-style of luxury.

What about being pointers? Are Christians doing any better in being a light to point others toward a Christian lifestyle? Not that I can observe. As mentioned, the national debt is a great problem. We berate our government officials for not doing something about it. We complain about inflation, which is what debt produces. About 90 percent of our inflation is directly related to the national debt, printing money to increase the money supply with no tangible securities to back it up. But as individuals we're not doing any better than our government. For several years the general trend in the United States has been to spend more money than is earned, about 10 percent more. Increasing debt by 10 percent annually isn't providing much of an example. Again, I don't observe that Christians are much different in this than others. We're not pointing others in the right direction.

Just *being legal* is not adequate for a Christian life-style: "Unless your righteousness surpasses that of the scribes and Pharisees, you shall not enter the kingdom of heaven" (Matt. 5:20). In the first place, as good as the laws of the land are it's possible to live just above the law and still be "crooked as a snake." Free enterprise has been distorted to the point that many interpret it to mean taking advantage of others for personal gain by manipulating the technicalities of the law. This philosophy has no place in Christian life-style.

In money management conferences, I encourage participants to enlist the help of a Christian financial advisor, attorney, or insurance agent when they need the expertise of such professionals. At one conference, a man reminded me that this approach sometimes fails. He related how a Sunday School teacher in his church, in one of these professions, had manipulated him through misrepresentation for personal gain but within the law. It's a sad day when a

Christian's life-style does not manifest itself in the market-place.

In the second place, there is no Christian growth in just being legal. If our objective is to attain legality, we can never progress beyond that point. This was the basis for Jesus' constant conflict with the Pharisees. They insisted that Jesus respond according to the law of Moses as they interpreted it. Evidently, that was not his purpose for coming into the world. His mission was to set men free, free to respond to God and be the image of God. This included freedom from the tyranny of law. Paul wrote, "It was for freedom that Christ set us free" (Gal. 5:1).

It is in this matter of law and freedom as it relates to growth that many Christians continue to have problems with their life-styles. Like the Pharisees, many Christians want upper limits on righteous living. They want to know how good they need to be for how long and still stay in God's grace or the church's grace.

This is particularly evident in giving, the area where many of us as church leaders have failed to rightly teach Christians. We set upper limits on Christian life-style when we apply the Old Testament law of tithing legalistically. I find no evidence in the New Testament that tithing should ever be taught as the final goal for Christian giving. When we teach this, that's where Christians stop growing in their giving. Or because it doesn't seem to be consistent with the love and free expression in Christ's teachings, they don't believe us in the first place.

We have also failed to teach Christians how to live and use material things. We have expressed more interest in the money members give than in how they live. Thus consumerism has shaped their life-styles, and we still expect them to be generous givers. Jesus clearly taught that our righteousness should exceed that of the Pharisees who were careful to give no more than a tithe. Paul concluded Galatians 5:1 by encouraging the Galatian Christians to "keep standing firm and do not be subject again to a yoke of slavery."

Growth is a necessary quality of Christian life-style: "Therefore you are to be perfect, as your heavenly Father is perfect" (Matt. 5:48). For many years I was told that Jesus said this because a lesser standard could not be set for Christians. If, for instance, he had said "try to be perfect," it would have provided a justifiable loophole and would have kept Christians from striving as hard. At the time it seemed logical, so I accepted it.

The Greek word translated here as "perfect" means mature or finished, and the verbs in the sentence are progressive. A more literal translation might read like this: "Be on your way toward becoming a finished, mature personality like God."[13] The growth idea contained here is the thrust of all New Testament teachings for Christians. We seem to have the idea that only secular life-style should be geared to upward mobility. But it's also true for Christian life-styles. Christian living, serving, and giving has perfection as its goal.

The Singleness of Purpose for Christian Life-style

Jesus taught that *purpose* is expressed by what we store up: "Do not lay up for yourselves treasures upon earth, where moth and rust destroy, and where thieves break in and steal" (Matt. 6:19). On and off, the whole sixth chapter of Matthew deals with material things, but verse 19 begins his key teaching on the subject. Here he teaches that values are determined by what we store up. It's not a condemnation of wealth but the examination of purpose. If one's security is in what's stored up, then a false set of values are determining life-style.

Being rich or poor is not the issue in this verse. A poor person can have just as much dependence upon material things as a rich person. The point is not to let material things determine your self-image. The advertisement asks, "What does your car say about you?" As we've seen, the thrust of secular life-style reduces people to objects and identifies objects as extensions of ourselves. This explains why we can get so angry when we lose, destroy, or someone steals our objects. We have confused our standard of living (quality and quantity of things) with our self-worth. That's what Jesus is saying not to let happen. There's no inherent security in storing up material things and identifying with them. When they rot, get eaten up, or stolen, our worth and identity go with them.

Our singleness of purpose is to develop a life-style which assures *permanent identity:* "Lay up for yourselves treasures in heaven, where neither moth nor rust destroys, and where thieves do not break in or steal" (Matt. 6:20). Mann helps us here also by pointing out that the desire for security is ultimately the desire for permanent existence or eternal identity.[14] Anonymity or the loss of identity is a real fear in our kind of secular society. To a great extent, our identity has been reduced to a Social Security number. And it's even worse when the numbers are reduced to some holes in a computer card. We get the feeling that selfhood is in danger of disappearing. Our computer card could get misplaced or punched wrong and we're gone—like the man recently who found out he was dead according to government records.

A few years ago after a mission conference in the association, I begin wrestling with a possible call to career mission work. After several months, I determined to my own satisfaction that God was not calling me at that time for that purpose. But only in recent years, while reflecting back on that experience, have I discovered why I was in so much agony at the time. It was a fear that I would be sent to some remote part of the world and be forgotten.

Jesus provides the answer to our identity problem: lay up treasures in heaven. How can we do this? Develop a life-style in the image of God. View life from God's management perspective. Have as your singleness of purpose enlarging God's kingdom. Eternal identity is built in; we're created in God's image. "If I honestly ask: 'Where is my security, whom or what do I trust and believe in?' And I reply, 'Jesus Christ . . .', I must then fully face the implications of believing in him and his gospel."[15] The security comes through obedience to Christ. God knew what our greatest need would be, and in his management of creation and salvation he made provisions for our permanent identity and security.

Christian Life-style as Witness

It's evident that everything we do is an expression of our chosen life-style. And every part of our life-style helps or hinders our Christian witness. Jesus teaches us not to have a *judgmental* life-style: "Do not judge lest you be judged. . . . why do you look at the speck in your brother's eye, but do not notice the log that is in your own eye? . . . Do not give what is holy to dogs, and do not throw your pearls before swine" (Matt. 7:1-6).

There's a question that unnerves me every time I think about it. When my neighbors observe my life-style—me, my family, our activities, car, house—is there anything noticeably Christian about it all? I'm conscious that if my life-style appears no different than my non-Christian neighbors, I have nothing unique to offer as evidence of my faith in Christ. It's not enough to drive by the non-Christian neighbor working in the yard on your way to church with a "look-how-holy-I-am" expression. The song "Let Others See Jesus in You" is more appropriate for shaping our life-styles. Our Christian management assignment requires that we reach out to them with our life, powers, influence, and resources.

Besides not having a judgmental life-style, our witness is made more effective by an evident *dependence upon God:* "If you then, being evil, know how to give good gifts to your children, how much more shall your Father who is in heaven give what is good to those who ask Him!" (Matt. 7:11). The verses just before this are about asking and receiving and giving your son bread instead of a rock when he asks. We have a fierce independence bred into us that reveals itself when we have to get spiritual about asking for help. We'll stand in line and let the government give to us but refuse to ask God. Sometimes I have this mental picture of a person coming into the world bucking and kicking like a wild horse screaming, "God, you'll never tame me." One of our best life-style witnesses is dependence upon God.

Just after my wife and I entered into our Christian money management commitment, I unexpectedly received a small rebate on some insurance. Since we had been exercising rigid management discipline the first two or three months in order to get our management plan going, I decided to encourage my wife to use the money for a new dress or something else she needed. Well, it didn't go as I had expected. When I surprised her with it, she started to cry. I thought, "It's not that big a thing!" But just that morning she had learned that a friend had a financial need and had prayed for some way to help her. The surprise rebate money provided her with the resources. Her dependence upon God was affirmed.

I don't want to overspiritualize this. God doesn't bail us out every time we pray for money. Good management is the each day's assignment which includes reasonable planning for the future. My point is this: if our non-Christian neighbors do not see in us an attitude of dependence upon God, they won't be nearly as apt to receive our verbal witness. If we grab and grasp for a living and have the same problems they're having, our witness is weak. The most beautiful life-styles I have observed are those of Christians who are observably dependent upon God's provisions.

Finally, *our own management life-style will be judged:* "compared to a wise man, who built his house upon the rock. . . . a foolish man, who built his house upon the sand" (Matt. 7:24-26). The results of our management follows us to the end. Those who are like the "house builder on the rock" understand the importance of relationships and the wise management of material things. The "house builder on the sand" didn't understand much about management. The contrast between the two reflects the difference in life-style choices.

I could wish that Columbus was right: "He who possesses gold does all that he wishes in this world, and succeeds in helping souls into paradise." The truth is, we devote most of our energy and resources to taking care of ourselves. In fact, we don't even take very good care of ourselves. Rather than acting intentionally, we spend much of our time reacting to crisis situations. We live mostly quiet, moral lives in which most of our attention and energy are given to ordinary daily details—food, clothes, transportation, family, friends, and doing for ourselves what we want.

It's not that the details of life must all be eradicated; they just need to be managed and given the proper priority. The great list of lesser things can seem much simpler when organized around Christ's purpose for our lives. It might be a good exercise to try to isolate the "thing" you most cherish and determine what would happen to you if you lost it. Or if it's an activity, what would you do if you could no longer participate in it. I'm sitting here typing with both hands. My present ministry requires that I spend much of my time doing just this. I've pondered the thought: *what if I should lose one hand or both?* I've used a lot of questions in the book because we need to be encouraged to make conscious choices.

To develop a Christian life-style, we must live intentional Christian lives. But there's little external support. Our secular culture teaches us to think and act only for ourselves; it reinforces the selfish human nature within us. The influence of dehumanization causes us to act more like animals than humans created in God's image. Self-preservation first and at all cost is an animal's response. Christian life-style knows a better way.

Many of us are less tempted by materialism than by satisfactions of prestige, power, or work itself. We carefully plan our lives, but minor tasks seem to take control. We seldom find time for some of the things which are most important.[16] So the greatest impact of our life-style choices is yet to be felt. There is nothing imaginary about the finite limits of natural resources. For future generations, we must find ways to crave less and use less rather than more. Life-style simplification is needed.

Notes

1. W. Everett Henry, "The American Notion of Wealth," *The Review and Expositor*, XXIX, 3 (July 1932), 285.

2. Joseph M. Dawson, "Sanctifying the Secular," *The Review and Expositor*, XLVII, 3 (July 1950), 304.

3. Donald E. Miller, "Life Style and Religious Commitment," *Religious Education* (January-February 1981), p. 57.

4. Charles A. Reich, *The Greening of America* (New York: Random House, 1970), p. 16.

5. Reich, p. 14.

6. John Francis Kavanaugh, *Following Christ in a Consumer Society: The Spirituality of Cultural Resistance* (Maryknoll, New York: Orbis Books, 1981), p. 21.

7. WSMV-TV, Nashville, Tennessee, July 7, 1983.

8. Kavanaugh, p. 40.

9. Miller, p. 57.

10. Cecil A. Ray, "Life-Style—Friend or Foe of Mission Support" (Unpublished paper, April 1976), p. 2.

11. Gerald Mann, *Why Does Jesus Make Me Nervous? Taking the Sermon on the Mount Seriously* (Waco, Texas: Word Books, 1980), p. 56.

12. David M. Beckmann, *Where Faith and Economics Meet: A Christian Critique* (Minneapolis: Augsburg Publishing House, 1981), pp. 103-102.

13. Mann, p. 95.

14. Mann, pp. 126-27.

15. Kavanaugh, p. 89.

16. Beckmann, p. 56.

4
Standard of Living and the Future

I was reared much like most others my age. Granted, we all have varied backgrounds—rural, village, town, city, Christian, non-Christian. Some of us were reared in a simple, agrarian setting where little money was exchanged for goods and services. Others were reared in the midst of a city and industry and exchanged money for almost every necessity of life.

My background happens to be rural, simple, and Christian. But in all of my preadult and early adult life I don't remember that the daily use of money and consumption of resources were related to being a Christian except perhaps morally. Some of you remember: don't gamble, don't buy whiskey, don't "blow" money foolishly. These moral adages applied to all people whether Christian or not; it was a matter of social reputation. Further, my childhood in the 1940s was guided by the colonial philosophy of consumption: "use it up, wear it out, make it do, or do without."

There is a much different philosophy in the use of money and consumption today. Industry tries to get us to spend as much money as possible. To create the need and desire are accomplished in two ways generally. Planned obsolescence (the length of time it takes for a product to wear out) is the first. You may have said, "They don't make'um like they used to," and they don't. Products are not made to last as

71

long as possible. They are made to wear out, thus creating a market for product replacement.

Second, desire is created and we are enticed to spend more money by an artificial obsolescence. This is advertising's job. An attitude is created that anything slightly old is slightly out of style and the obviously new is more fashionable and more desirable. This widespread waste of energy and resources has become an American habit to generate profits.[1]

I was not aware until recent years that such a general philosophy in industry had programmed my standard of living to want the new and the better. A former marketing employee with a major appliance manufacturer illustrated for me how industry planned ahead to accomplish this. Using the refrigerator as an example, they started with a basic unit. In the next year or two, they introduced a new model with an ice maker and used advertising to create consumer need (want). They knew how to make ice makers when they put the basic unit on the market. In fact, they probably already knew how they could include a cold water dispenser, ice dispenser, juice dispenser, and digital display showing the temperature. But you can't create as large of a market by putting them all on at once. So they schedule them every year or two.

In much the same way, I was not aware as a child and young adult that the use of money and material things was related to being a Christian. But this doesn't mean that it's a new idea, that industry's philosophy is just another acceptable choice based on personal preference. The use of wealth has everything to do with Christian commitment. The fact is, Christians and the church have been guided at times by principles which are not Christian.

We need to evaluate the secular principles of quantity of consumption and luxury of goods and services; if continued, we need to determine the impact on future generations. The previous chapter illustrated how we often unintentionally become immoral in our life-styles. Undisciplined life-style was compared to Christ's teachings about disciplined living. It dealt with everyday moral relationships with people and things, and how one influences the other. This chapter takes a wider view, a world view. It looks at how our standard of living influences the rest of the world now as well as our children's future.

Standard of living is one expression of life-style. As indicated in the previous chapter, standard of living specifically includes choices of quantity and quality. In the survey which follows, I will explore different expressions and consequences of our choices and, last, some basis for making right choices.

Choices of Quantity and Quality

What has nearly thirty years of intense, planned, and contrived overconsumption and luxury created? A look at what has prompted our choices will help to illustrate what has happened.

Progress

One measure of progress is increased quantity and quality. From infancy, we are programmed that progress is based on the amount of money we can make and the volume of things we can acquire. Education is one example. A major goal of education is progress; "If you don't get a good education, you'll never amount to anything." From the times of the Old Testament, it has been evident that acquiring knowledge and wisdom is good. It helps us become all that God created us to be. But we tend to translate it differently; education means personal success, greater wealth, and thus progress. An equal and balanced emphasis on using increased knowledge to serve God and humanity better is often ignored.

More is better. The wealthy become the role models. Industry uses consumerism to exploit our egos and tell us that what's good for industry is good for the country. Craving for more becomes patriotism and consumption a citizen's duty in order to insure continued progress.

We are programmed to accept greed as being normal; greed contributes to progress according to the secular philosophy of progress. And few of us are immune to the temptation dangled before us constantly. For example, many of us otherwise fairly disciplined folks yield to the sweepstakes offers which promise to make us millionaires. As a Christian you may have rationalized and baptized your participation, as I have done, by promising God that if you win you'll give him half (well, maybe a fourth but certainly no less than a tenth). Clinical psychologists Goldberg and Lewis have pointed out that "the lure of instant riches is an opiate that dulls reasoning and common sense."[2] But it's hard for us to see it that way. More money is progress, our progress. As much as we detest manipulation, we let ourselves be manipulated by industry for the chance to have more.

Generally, we think of progress as more and better of everything. Progress is more and better speed, comfort, knowledge, and health. The prevailing attitude is that having progress in these four areas is worth whatever it takes, even if it means mortgaging the future. Our standard of measure is prosperous Mr. and Ms. America. Our national heroes are those who excel in one or more of the big four areas of progress. We organize labor unions, lobby politicians, and hold demonstrations for the sake of progress. Perish the thought that such freedoms should be denied. But they should be used responsibly. This is just to point out that many of our choices are influenced by a contrived attitude of need and want. A fifty-billion-dollar-a-year advertising industry has seen to it that our natural craving for progress is kept healthy and active.

Ironically, our desire for progress has biblical roots as Christian economist and World Bank member David Beckmann has illustrated.[3] Mankind's first management assignment contained the element of progress: subdue and rule over, cultivate and care for the garden (Gen. 1:28; 2:15). The history of God's dealings with people from creation to Christ's coming in glory is based on progress. Abraham was to be a blessing to all nations. The Israelites in Egypt anticipated deliverance. Prosperity was always in the Lord. The prophets promised a new age when God's people would obey him as they looked for the Messiah. The progress Christ promises is beyond imagination. Not only are the dead going to be resurrected, the whole world will be redeemed from decay (Rom. 8).

As is so often true, an innate and God-given longing has been misdirected. Like Lot (Gen. 13) and Judas (Mark 14), many of our choices for more and better are for the wrong purpose or for the wrong things. We may be sacrificing our humanity and the future for the sake of our progress.

Energy

Progress, especially in the secular sense, depends upon energy. The quantity and quality of resources we have chosen to use are staggering. "The U.S. consumes 33 percent of nonrenewable energy and mineral resources. . . . Yet the population of the U.S. is only 6.2 percent of the total world population."[4] Sheaffer and Brand, environmental consultant and biology professor respectively, note:

The greatest nation in the world—leader in scientific

achievement, industrial production, and military strength—
faces a momentous problem: a scarcity of the energy that
helped power it to preeminence. More than any other nation,
the United States depends on prodigious quantities of energy
to create climate-controlled enclosures, power industrial op-
erations, transport people and goods, and produce food.
Once-cheap fossil fuels are moving toward the precious
commodity category, forcing policy makers in energy,
finance, and politics to make crucial decisions about power
sources for the future. Their actions not only affect the avail-
ability of energy ten years from now but the health and
living standard of energy users tomorrow. But the experts
disagree on national energy policies.[5]

Such discussions about energy seem far removed from the
average citizen who works hard to get ahead, plays hard to
enjoy what he has earned, and anticipates a future of plenty
with more and better conveniences. As the spendthrift who
awoke one day to discover that he had depleted his resources, we got a jolt in 1973 when the first Middle East oil
embargo was imposed. Two things happened: the cost of
living was dramatically increased, and we were made aware
that energy from nonrenewable resources was finite. But our
lesson was short-lived. We grew accustomed to paying the
higher prices for luxuries and went back to unconscious
consumption of energy. In 1978-79 it happened again: tem-
pers flared when forced changes altered the way Americans
lived.

Declining sources of energy and more expensive energy
forced industry to change, a change which could just as
easily have been made years before but was not as profitable. For example, smaller and more fuel efficient cars could
have been produced years before. But consumers didn't
want to change their standard of living—a "bigger is better
mentality." Many other similar modifications occurred in

the 1970s and early 1980s. These forced alterations have
changed attitudes about energy consumption, but I don't see
any great difference in the overall philosophy of life and
expectations. Changes in industry and personal adjustments
appear to be more a matter of economics than of Christian
stewardship. Basically, the belief prevails: "If I have the
money to pay for what I want, I have the right to consume
as much as I desire." Changes are viewed as necessary incon-
veniences rather than an opportunity to excel as God's assigned managers.

Christians and churches are equally guilty of unnecessary
and extravagant energy consumption. A survey of church
facilities and activities will reveal that the choices Christians
have made in the recent past were without regard for energy
conservation. During the 1950s when energy was cheap,
spacious and fine facilities were a means to increased
growth. In the eighties, large, uninsulated facilities consume
a disproportionate amount of financial resources of a con-
gregation. The idea of reaching people whatever the cost has
had to be reevaluated. Suddenly, bigger and more may be a
hindrance rather than a help.

As with industry and with individuals, churches have
been forced to change their standard of living. But as I travel
around the nation, many of the changes I observe some
churches making are not the best ones. Rather than making
more energy efficient buildings and adapting programming,
they're cutting back on quality training and activities necessary to outreach and mission support by allocating more
resources for energy. In other words, churches are reacting
to the crisis by changing figures on paper rather than physi-
cally becoming more efficient.

Effective Christian management of energy resources
should precede necessity and law. But as a second best, if we
fail in the first instance and if necessity and law must be

used, then Christians should be the first and best participants. Apart from the impact that wasteful depletion of oil,
coal, and natural gas (fossil fuels) will have on future generations, there is an immediate impact. On a personal and
family level, as with churches, the more money spent on
energy the less money available for Christian work and service. The results will be a further decline in the influence of
Christianity on the world for good. This negates God's management assignment to us in both the Old and New Testa-
ments. The standard of living we have chosen is consuming
a disproportionate amount of energy beyond physical
necessities. We can't support our present choice of life-
styles and still fulfill the Great Commission.

An even greater reason for frustration over excessive consumption is the fact that present standards could be continued on 30 to 50 percent less energy than is currently being
used. I'm certainly not perfect in conservation, but by
retrofitting and being sensitive to energy use I'm spending
a lesser dollar amount to heat, cool, and light my house now
than in 1978. (I have an all-electric house except for a small
kerosene portable heater.) To accomplish this apart from
routine maintenance, I've spent less than $1000 for insula-
tion and other changes. Without any noticeable inconveni-
ences to standard of living in this regard and based on
increases in the cost of energy, I've reduced energy cost more
than 50 percent. It's a matter of consciously applying management principles.

Poverty, Food, Health, and Illiteracy

Poverty, lack of food, poor health, and illiteracy have
been combined because of their close relationship. Poverty
inevitably creates low nutrition and poor health, and illiteracy is a prime contributor to the other three. And though
discussed separately, energy prices are also a critical factor

in all four areas. Together, they prevent a large portion of the world's population from achieving their God-given physical and mental capabilities.

Poverty is measured in four ways: "relative inequality of income, absolute poverty, differentiated economic and social factors, and nutrition."[6] Relative inequality of income is the difference in per capita income of nations. For example, per capita income in the United States in 1974 was 22 times greater than 26 nations, and 8.8 times greater than 28 other nations. Of 105 nations reporting at that time, only 25 had per capita incomes over $2,000 compared to $6,600 in the United States.[7]

Absolute poverty relates to basic needs for food, shelter, health, and education. Accuracy in counting is difficult, but it is estimated that of the world's more than 4.4 billion population, over one-half billion (perhaps 800 million) people are absolutely poor.[8] That is, these basic needs are going unmet. The result is an extremely high mortality rate with life expectancy little more than one half that in the United States. In reality, poverty equals death. The mortality rate of children overall in Nigeria is 40 percent compared to 3 percent in the United States.[9] Even in our country, more than 10 percent of the people live below the government established poverty level. However, in most cases this is still considerably better than the condition of the poor in many Third World countries.

Differentiated economic and social factors, the third measure of poverty, "is maintained by social and political power, exercised in a framework of human relationships."[10] Law enforces the continuing division between the poor and affluent. Essentially, illiteracy among the poor creates a situation in which they know no better than to support the affluent who enforce the laws that oppress them. When the political system offers no options, people simply become expressions of the culture they have inherited. They are not able to analyze their situation and respond, and thus are vulnerable to the exploits of government, the educated, and the wealthy.

The most devastating effect of poverty is the lack of nutrition. Though inadequate nutrition is involved in the measure of absolute poverty, its impact is so great on the poor that it must stand alone as the fourth measure of poverty. Because of frequent media coverage, we are aware of the malnourished people of the world with children being affected most. It was noted earlier that perhaps 800 million people of the world are absolutely poor, with inadequate diets. Probably another 500 million or more don't have enough food to meet their basic bodily needs.[11] We tend to think of world hunger as being somewhere else, India or Bangladesh. But according to a recent congressional sub-committee study and report, one in seven people in the United States is hungry.[12]

Illiteracy is a major reason for poverty, malnourishment, and poor health. Generally, countries with high rates of poverty and hunger have high rates of illiteracy and mortality. Exceptions do occur during times of war and nature-related calamities. Illiteracy in countries such as Upper Volta, West Africa, is over 90 percent. Those of us who have visited one or more of these countries are appalled at the rampant sickness and disease. Even in the United States, it is estimated that there are 24 million functional illiterates. Being illiterate and being poor are often companion maladies.

The redistribution of actual wealth in the world in order to reduce poverty is not a foreseeable human possibility. However, great reduction in malnutrition, poor health, and illiteracy are more within the scope of human response. To reduce malnutrition would contribute to the reduction of the other two. That's not to say that specific medical and literacy work wouldn't be needed, but the inner relationships are obvious.

Using world hunger as an example, what is the prognosis? The first consideration must be life-style choices regarding quantity and quality of consumption. Here in the United States, we spend more for products to take off weight than some countries spend to put it on. We feed our dogs a more nutritious diet than a fourth of the world's people are fed.[13] (We even have diet food for overweight dogs.) The intent is not to try to create guilt because we have a more than adequate diet; rather it's to create a perspective.

As with fossil fuels, food supplies are finite. It is estimated that to bring all people in the world to our level of diet would require a fourfold increase in the land's productivity.[14] That possibility is unlikely under present management systems. The land in cultivation simply will not tolerate that kind of sustained production.

But there are alternatives. For example, growing grain to feed livestock has a 10 percent protein efficiency. When grain is fed to livestock, by the time it's converted into beef about 90 percent of the original protein has been lost.[15] If, instead, the grain is eaten directly, many more people could be fed from the same amount of land. (Excess grain, when available, could continue to be fed to livestock to produce higher quality and more palatable protein.)

Granted, there is more involved in providing food for the world than not feeding grain to livestock. The production of food involves many other related areas of management— soil, water, and energy management in particular. Then there is the ever-troublesome problem of conglomerate landowners who plant cash crops in the very countries of need and sell the harvest to multinational corporations while native workers go hungry.[16] National and international politics also contribute to the problem.

But as Christians we are called to be sensitive to the needs of the world's people. Secular management seldom looks for more than a gradual alleviation of poverty. But the Bible teaches us to hope and work for the end of suffering, sin, and degradation of people. Though we can't personally solve all of the problems in the world which contribute to poverty, poor nutrition, ill health, and illiteracy, we can work on our own problem of overconsumption. Consumer choices can change economics. (Remember the Edsel?) We can become aware of the forces which create much of the desire to consume. Consumerism wants us to be ignorant of the poor and disenfranchised people lest we give our money away instead of spending it on luxuries which generate profits.

It is evident that we or our children will have to readjust the diet of natural resources and food to which we have become accustomed. As Christians, we must choose whether that change will be forced upon us, or whether we will be leaders in initiating it. Standard of living choices can't be ignored forever.

Examples of extravagant and wasteful use of resources for the sake of profit and luxury are themselves destructive. But the devastation caused by our standard of living choices is accelerated when we observe the continuing deterioration of the natural order.

Choices and the Future

Christian management has a future orientation. In contrast, poverty has a "today" orientation. Goldberg and Lewis point out, for example, that "successful investment depends on the ability to forecast developmental trends, to predict the future growth. It involves the principle of planning for the future, of putting off immediate gratification in favor of long-term rewards."[17] Since hungry people can't think beyond their hunger, it's unreasonable to expect them to put off immediate gratification in favor of long-term rewards.

This successful investment principle, when placed in a Christian context, is applicable to Christian management and responsibility. From Scripture, Christians have been schooled with a future orientation. And in much of the Western world, we have been blessed with more than enough resources. But too often we have responded as the poor in seeking immediate gratification without regard for future needs because of our greed. Or we expect that the end is near, so it won't matter what kind of shape we leave the world in anyway. Both attitudes thwart Christian management and produce the same poor results. Each irresponsible management decision further deteriorates our absolute livelihood and our ability to respond to the needs of the world's people. This can be seen in the way we are treating our natural resources.

The Once Good Earth

Satisfying physical needs and wants takes energy. It's estimated that 96 percent of the energy used worldwide is produced from fossil fuels.[18] With the exception of solar, water, and wind power, the use of energy takes away from the earth's resources. Multiply the daily needs and wants of more than 4.4 billion people in the world and the speed of resource depletion becomes incomprehensible. To meet the growing demand for energy, large portions of the natural environment have been mutilated and the ecological balance disrupted. Until recent years, little attention has been given to future goals as we have sought to gratify present demands.

We have responded much like Hatter in Lewis Carroll's

Alice in Wonderland as Alice questioned him about the use of natural resources.

> "Then you keep moving around, I suppose?"
> said Alice.
> "Exactly so", said the Hatter, "As the things get
> used up."
> "But when you come to the beginning again?"
> Alice ventured to ask.
> "Suppose we change the subject," the March Hare
> interrupted, yawning. "I'm getting tired
> of this."[19]

For fear of having to change our way of living, we too have tried to ignore the effects of our pillage of the earth.

The Ecological Balance. —When God created the earth and placed us in charge of it, there was a perfect ecological balance. In his book *Earthkeeping,* Loren Wilkinson and his colleagues at Trinity College report on studies which have singled out what is called ecosystems (a set of interacting plants, animals, and nonliving things—such as earth, water, and wind—which can be viewed as a functioning unity).[20] In natural ecosystems, a perfect cycle of plant and animal nurture and decay is maintained; living things live within limits. They have no outside sources of energy to draw from, so they must and do live on what they have. In nature, living things rarely exploit their resources to the extent that they collapse.

In our quest for more energy resources, the destruction of natural ecosystems is reaching alarming proportions. Though recent environmental laws require industries who provide energy resources to restore the land, the original ecosystem can never be replaced. It may seem rather inconsequential that a few varieties of plants will never grow on the same land again, or that a few species of animals will never return to the restored area. But when this happens, nature is unbalanced. The net result is a population explosion of some pest, plant, or animal, which was controlled before by something which was removed from the original ecosystem.

This is especially true when the natural habitats of birds are destroyed, resulting in their death or migration to another area. The insect population usually increases and reduces the crop production unless insecticides are used. The production of insecticides requires more energy, causes pollution, and the cost of agricultural products are increased.

Only human beings, of all God's creation, have the ability to change the natural order to such a degree. Loren Eisely, an anthropologist, reflects on human manipulation of nature.

> It is with the coming of man that a vast hole seems to open in nature, a vast black whirlpool spinning faster and faster, consuming flesh, stones, soil, minerals . . . wrenching power from the atom, until the ancient sounds of nature are drowned . . . something which is no longer nature . . . something demonic and no longer planned . . . contending in a final giant's game against its master.[21]

Soil Conservation. —Crop-producing land is a human-managed ecosystem. As the world population expanded, humans required more food than could be acquired from hunting, fishing, and gathering from the wild. At first, when land was cleared for cultivation, the natural organic material provided sufficient nutrients for producing food crops. And the level of production necessary was not very demanding; usually a family provided only for itself. With urbanization came greater demands for food to be supplied by farmers to nonfarmers. To increase productivity (and profits), commercial fertilizers were used. As labor costs increased, mechanized farming accelerated. Farming became big business and efficiency took precedence over conservation. Again, short-term results were sought without a long-term view of future needs.

Farmlands are becoming dust bowls, and much of the valuable topsoil—exposed to wind and rain unprotected—is being lost.

> The result, almost without exception, is that we have replaced ecosystems which had a yearly gain in topsoil with systems which have a yearly loss in topsoil. The complex natural system made up of many plants and animals has been replaced by simple systems with only one or two components. Self-regulating features have thus been destroyed; vital nutrients no longer recycle with the system, but escape to rivers, lakes, oceans, and the atmosphere.[22]

Every loss in the natural rebuilding cycle places greater demands on already dwindling energy supplies.

Careless depletion of the soil's nutrients has been increased by nonresident ownership of farmlands. Investors buy land for speculation and lease it to corporate farmers. Poorer conservation results when nonowners cultivate the land. They are motivated more by immediate profits than long-range management. (Have you noticed how new rental cars are often abused?)

The Once Good Environment

All energy consumption of fossil fuels produces pollution —air, water, soil, and noise pollution. As I write today, pollution has reduced visibility at the airport to one-and-one-half miles, and I don't live in an industrial city. For many of us, however, Love Canal, Three Mile Island, and Times Beach are far removed, isolated incidents which couldn't happen in our area. Acid rain and nuclear waste are frequent news subjects. In the sprawling cities, the crickets and birds are seldom heard.

Industrial Pollution. —As children do, industries in the past (and some still) tend to see how much pollution they can get away with before they get their hands slapped. Similar to people in mass, large industries often don't respond to the affects of pollution with sensitivity. In the name of progress, to satisfy consumer demands, and to increase profits, industries have and are producing billions of tons of pollution.

Air pollution from the use of fossil fuels poses a threat to all forms of life in many industrial areas. Sheaffer and Brand point out some of the effects of two of the most troublesome air pollutants.[23] Sulfur dioxide produced from burning coal and gasoline is particularly destructive. Concentrations of sulfur dioxide produce acid rain which increases soil acidity, reduces or eliminates plant growth, and contaminates fresh water lakes. Among many other air pollutants, ozone is another especially dangerous gas produced by fossil fuel combustion. It impairs respiration in people and animals and damages plant growth. This is only a part of the price we are paying for progress.

Waste products dumped directly into water and on the land are equally dangerous to the life of living things. Hardly a week passes without reports of fish kills, illegal dumping of chemicals, accidental nuclear spills, dioxin and PCB contamination, and traces of chemical pesticides found in animals as far away as penguins in Antarctica. Many of these pollutants contain carcinogens which cause cancer, others cause liver and cardiovascular disease, some affect the nervous system, and more. Wherever pollution exists, quality of life is diminished. Industry is by far the largest polluter but not the only one.

Consumer Pollution. —Ordinary, otherwise decent folk also contribute to our pollution problem. Similar to the insensitivity of industry, we tend to rationalize that pollution is someone else's problem. We complain about the fish kills and the contamination, but that's industry's fault and the government's problem. We reason that the little bit of trash we dump won't amount to anything or that driving 55 miles per hour is for those whose work is less important than ours.

When such an irresponsible attitude is multiplied by several million people, the bad results affect every one. I was made very aware of just such a situation a short time ago while revisiting Saratoga Lake. Twenty-one years earlier while living in Saratoga Springs, New York, I had enjoyed fishing, boating, and skiing in the lake. The water was beautiful. Seeing the lake on my recent visit there was depressing. In the intervening twenty-one years it had become a cesspool. Trash cluttered the surface. And though it was a beautiful, warm day, people were conspicuously absent. Hundreds of other lakes and streams have fallen prey to similar user abuse in the past twenty years.

Many people have a blatant disrespect for nature. It seems even more disrespectful when adult Christians practice such abuse. I have seen adult church members throw the trash from a fast-food restaurant onto the church parking lot—paper sack, hamburger container, drink cup, and napkin. Highways, streets, and parks are littered with debris. I can better understand farmers' abuse of the land to reduce the cost of production or industry's pollution to provide less expensive goods than I can understand the reckless way individuals treat their natural environment. The farmers and industry are producing usable commodities and getting a return on their labor. Private polluters, on the other hand, create problems for others and additional expense in taxes to clean up after them.

This overview of indiscriminate consumption and luxury resulting in depletion and destruction of the natural order shows how the whole world is affected. What I have shared is superficial and nontechnical. There are hundreds of books and research reports on each of the subject areas I have mentioned, and many other subjects just as important have been omitted.

My purpose is to illustrate the need for an immediate and sustained Christian management response. Every decision we make to increase our quantity of goods and services and/or raise the quality of our material existence usually further decreases energy resources, increases pollution, reduces the possibility of helping hurting humanity, and more. But for every problem which has been raised, there is a Christian response.

Christians' Response

Except for faith in God's work of redemption through Christ, it's hard to be optimistic about the future. I noticed that after doing research for this chapter, I became annoyed and somewhat depressed. I lost my drive; there was an urge to withdraw. But then, when I started to concentrate on what some Christians are doing and what all of us can do, the drive to continue returned. The management assignment God gave to us contains the purpose and motive we need for living and serving.

But where do we start? The magnitude of the problem is so great. A poster showing a baby chick just hatched expresses my feelings sometimes. With the chick standing beside the broken egg shell from which it has just emerged, the caption has the chick asking, "What do I do now?"

In chapters 1 and 2 I discussed the biblical basis for a Christian management response to all of life. Though it was not stated directly, the discussion related to Christian doctrine: the doctrine of God, man, creation, and management (stewardship). Doctrine is the place to begin when considering standard of living choices. The following discussion is about how doctrine is applied in daily choices.

Commitment

Christian commitment is related to growth. A personal commitment to Christ does not ensure that a new Christian will automatically know how to think and live. Patterns for Christian living develop as a person grows in understanding Christ's teachings. The first responsibility of a new Christian is to learn what the Bible teaches about living as a Christian —Bible study, worship, and prayer. Like automatic responses required to drive a car comfortably, we must learn to respond automatically to situations which demand a Christian management response.

Knowing something to the point of automatic response usually takes conscious effort. This is a further responsibility in Christian life-style development. After making an open commitment to Christ as Savior, a person must desire to be a Christian manager. It is this desire that leads to a specific, conscious commitment to a Christian life-style. The life-style commitment provides the sensitivity necessary to recognize the manipulation of secularism and counter its influence.

As John wrote to the young Christians in his day, "Test the spirits to see whether they are from God" (1 John 4:1). To dare question the spirit of secularism requires Christian intelligence and commitment. If the choice has not already been made to be a Christian manager before confronting standard of living decisions, the wrong decision is more apt to be made than not. Christian commitment comes before Christian choices and actions.

Attitude

Our attitude about our standard of living not only guides our life-style choices, it is itself a choice we make. Viktor Frankl, a German theologian and writer, wrote from a World War II concentration camp that attitude is one thing no person can take away from another.[24] We can choose the attitude we will have in any particular circumstance. This agrees with Scripture. Paul encouraged the Philippian Christians to "Have this attitude in yourselves which was also in Christ Jesus" (Phil. 2:5). That is, choose to have the attitude of a servant (Phil. 2:7).

Attitude precedes action. In all decisions that involve our relationship to wealth, our God-given mental and spiritual abilities make it possible to choose to have a Christian or secular attitude. If we have a Christian attitude, standard of living choices will be made in terms of conservation, ecology, and ministry to the world's people. If we have a secular attitude, choices will be selfish and without regard for Christian management principles. Every person "owns" his own attitude.

Though our attitude toward abundance and luxury can and should be consciously chosen, competing secular influences can develop unconscious attitudes also. Unconscious attitudes, unexamined and unchallenged, often motivate particular kinds of life-styles that are difficult to manage. For most of us who are seeking to live a Christian life-style, there is a constant struggle between purer conscious desires and unconscious attitudes. Jesus teaches us that we cannot serve both God and money. (See Matt. 6:24.) However, the majority of what most of us hear, read, and observe each day contradicts Jesus' teachings. We live in a tension between the two. The term *secular Christians* describes people who try to have both secular and Christian standards of living.

Values

As with attitude, values are personal property. And, like attitude, values can be developed. For Christians, the Scriptures provide the standard by which value choices are evaluated. But Christians and non-Christians alike can be motivated by trends, fads, consumerism, and other influences.

By definition, the word *value* identifies strength and worth. This could be anything from the strength of purchasing power, to integrity, to depth of commitment to a person or doctrine. The word *value* is normally understood to be positive—the worth of a thing, high standards, quantity, and quality. In common usage, however, this is not always true. The phrase "value choices" suggests that there are more than one set of values.

Two opposite sets of values are identified in the Bible: godly and worldly. Paul wrote Titus, "For the grace of God that bringeth salvation hath appeared to all men, Teaching us that, denying ungodliness and worldly lusts, we should live soberly, righteously, and godly, in this present world" (Titus 2:11-12, KJV).

Godly values are inherent in the nature of God and expressed in his creation and relationship to us. All that God does is for the benefit of people. But worldly values are established apart from any consideration of God—they are selfish; they are created in our minds and have no greater worth than our finiteness. Although God creates us with the freedom to choose between the greater and lesser values, God is honored only when the greater values are chosen. Thus when we choose Christian values we please God.

But value choices have always been a problem for people. Based on the choices of Adam and Eve, Cain, Lot, Judas, Ananias and Sapphira, and us, it appears that persons come into the world bent on making selfish value choices. That is not to say that Christians never make godly choices, we just have trouble making them consistently. Secular values are an ever-present enticement: "Every man is tempted, when he is drawn away of his own lust, and enticed. Then when lust hath conceived, it bringeth forth sin: and sin when it is finished, bringeth forth death" (Jas. 1:14-15, KJV). In this way we are entrapped by the world's values.

At the highest level, value choices are commitments to principles or doctrine. We are seldom tempted to first deny God by accepting false doctrine. Rather, something material draws us away from God. In isolation, our management of God's world is for ourselves instead of for God and others. In this we have accepted the world's doctrine of secularism, organizing life without God. Since our doctrinal commitments determine our value choices, choosing worldly values is inevitable when separated from God.

It's a sobering thought but an obvious conclusion: what we do with what we have is a true measure of our hope for our future physical and spiritual life.

Notes

1. John R. Sheaffer and Raymond H. Brand, *Whatever Happened to Eden?* (Wheaton, Illinois: Tyndale House, Publishers, Inc., 1980), pp. 112-13.

2. Herb Goldberg and Robert T. Lewis, *Money Madness: The Psychology of Saving, Spending, Loving, and Hating Money* (New York: The New American Library, Inc., 1978), p. 196.

3. Beckmann, pp. 39-50.

4. Loren Wilkinson, ed., *Earthkeeping: Christian Stewardship of Natural Resources* (Grand Rapids: William B. Eerdmans Publishing Company, 1980), p. 80.

5. Sheaffer and Brand, p. 69.

6. George S. Siudy, Jr., "Stewardship and World Poverty," *The Earth Is The Lord's: Essays on Stewardship,* eds. Mary Evelyn Jegen and Bruno V. Manno (New York: Paulist Press, 1978), p. 149.

7. Ibid, p. 149.

8. Beckmann, pp. 81-82.
9. Siudy, p. 150-51.
10. Siudy, p. 150.
11. Wilkinson, p. 39.
12. Reported by ABC-TV World News Tonight, July 8, 1983.
13. Kavanaugh, p. 18.
14. Wilkinson, p. 39.
15. Wilkinson, p. 36.
16. Sheaffer and Brand, pp. 123-24.
17. Goldberg and Lewis, p. 188-89.
18. Sheaffer and Brand, p. 70.
19. Wilkinson, p. 49.
20. Wilkinson, pp. 12-13.
21. Wilkinson, p. 15
22. Wilkinson, p. 16.
23. Sheaffer and Brand, p. 29.
24. Viktor Frankl, *Man's Search for Meaning* (New York: Simon and Schuster, 1963), p. 104.

Part
3
How to Manage for Christian Living

5
Management Planning: Goals and Income

The material in chapters 1 through 4 is my justification for a commitment to and the practice of Christian money management. But your commitment can't be based on my justification. You must arrive at your own reason why. Mine is based on the thesis of this book: God placed persons in charge of his world, and those who accept Christ as Savior have a unique management responsibility to continue his redemptive activity. This has resulted in my commitment to the biblical principles of management. It was biblical doctrine and commitment that changed the direction of my family's money management.

After a commitment to the biblical doctrine, managing for Christian living begins with planning. It involves objectives, goals, and actions. For most of us, planning for our daily money management needs to be kept simple, especially in the beginning. To help simplify the planning process here, I'm going to assume three objectives for all Christians. In your own planning, you may want to make these more specific.

1. To share the gospel of Christ to enlarge his kingdom.
2. To provide adequately for oneself and one's family.

3.   To be a responsible citizen of the community, state, and country where you live, which includes helping those in need.

After objectives have been decided upon in the planning process, goals are chosen which will help accomplish those objectives. Assuming that you have accepted my objectives, choosing your goals is the *first step* in developing your personal or family money management plan.

Choosing Your Goals

I'm convinced that lack of conscious thought given to goal setting is a major cause of mismanagement for many Christians. If an attempt is made to construct a management plan, it's usually a survival plan. We begin by determining our income and estimating our expenses. The goal is to balance the two. Since so many American families live from one payday to the next, it's obvious that survival is the number one goal. Planning for the majority of people, then, is for no more than one or two weeks in advance except in a few no option areas: Social Security, company pension plans, and perhaps insurance.

Why do we dislike setting goals? Different people probably have different reasons. I didn't think I made enough money to justify setting goals. My wife thought of goals and a budget as restrictive. For whatever reason we may resist goal setting, it can be a rewarding experience, especially after a few successes in reaching goals. Those who succeed are willing to do what they dislike, at least for a time, because they know it's right rather than because it feels good. In time, however, having goals does feel good; it's good to know where you're going. Someone has said that "the world steps aside to let the person by who knows where he's going." That's the kind of disciplined example Christians need to provide for the world in money matters.

There are some basic guidelines for Christians when setting goals. Keep in mind your purpose for being in the world; you're God's representative, God's manager. So think of your goal setting as reverently daydreaming. (For this exercise, forget about your income. Goals and income can be compared later.) Though most of your goals will be personal and/or family related, they are nonetheless for God's sake. Your goals will usually benefit the whole family if you're married, and they will contribute to your growth in Christian life-style. Each goal is a bite-sized piece in becoming a more perfect Christian disciple. To reach our goals is often choosing to forego lesser, temporary gratification in order to obtain greater, more permanent contentment.

Further, it's usually best to divide your goals into three categories: next year, the next five years, and long-range goals (five to twenty years or more). The wisdom of this approach should be evident in the discussion which follows. Goal illustrations will come from that first year when my wife and I made our commitment to Christian money management.

Goals for Next Year

Goals should start where you are, with your present needs. Some of them may appear trivial, but include them anyway. Some goals may be corrective, clearing up a past bad-management decision. Others will be preventive, a stopgap measure to keep a bad situation from getting worse. However, some of your goals should be challenging; they should stretch your ability. But no goal, if it helps you become more effective in money management, is insignificant. All goals for next year, when accomplished, contribute to future successes; some of them will be the first step toward a longer-range and more important goal—like starting a plan for savings. Note the following goals in my family's planning that first year.

Pay cash for supplies to paint the house.—Painting the house without buying the paint with credit seems a rather small thing. As I recall, it cost less than $100. But previously, it would have been purchased with credit; no other method would have been considered. This goal was among the first we accomplished. I bought the paint on sale with real money and did the painting myself. Such small, satisfying experiences often provide the needed motivation to tackle more challenging goals.

Reduce installment debt.—Hopefully, this is not a problem for you. Over a twenty-one-year period of almost continuous use and abuse of revolving credit, I had amassed an unmanageable balance of about 21 percent of my spendable income. (The twenty-one years and 21 percent are a coincidence.) Because of many consolidation loans, I didn't even know for what much of the balance was owed. I had little freedom to purchase goods and services at the least expensive places or to take advantage of seasonal sales unless it happened to be at one of the places where I could use credit.

To begin a workable management plan, it was necessary once again for me to consolidate the various sources of credit. But out of my experience, consolidation should be considered the least effective of all solutions. The best action to reduce installment debt is to stop charging and concentrate on paying off debts. When one account is paid in full, apply the monthly amount of that payment to the account which you will pay off next. The accelerated repayment rate may surprise you.

Another tactic in reducing installment debt, if this is one of your goals, is to apply any unexpected income to debt repayment. I used gifts of money and small honorariums for this purpose, money which in the past had been spent indiscriminately. (Many people receive some amount of such money each year.) When there is a consciously chosen goal toward which you're working, using incidental income for that purpose is not a sacrifice but a joy. When debt is not a problem, such surplus money can be used in many other meaningful ways rather than raising one's standard of living.

Our goal was to eliminate installment debt in three years, but it had to be a one-year goal repeated three times. For those of us who tend to be impatient, three years may seem a long time to work at such an unpleasant task. But considering that I had been working twenty-one years accumulating debts, three years was a relatively short turnaround period. And it was not a three-year sacrifice. Within three or four months, combining this part of the management plan with the others, the sense of sacrifice begin to subside. The greatest joy came when in two years and seven months the last payment was made, five months ahead of schedule.

Begin savings (an emergency fund).—My previous attempts at saving money had lasted a month or two at best. There was no plan or goal; I had only tried to save any money that might be considered extra at a given time. In reality there was no extra money at any time because there was no accumulated money to use as a buffer for fluctuating, ongoing family expenses.

In our management plan, we set a specific, though small, amount to be placed in savings each month. The first major use of the emergency fund was about nine months into the plan. One of our cars was totaled in an accident. The second major use came a year later when I had to replace the roof on the house. This was another project I did myself and was able to pay cash for the materials. Even with these and other uses, it has continued to accumulate. (Saving for emergencies and long-range savings are discussed more fully in chapter 7.)

A major area of our savings plan involved the children's college. One of the three children was in college and the other two were approaching college age. No provisions had been made for their college expenses. The best we could do was a stopgap measure as I mentioned earlier. This required that we set a goal and channel as much money as possible into the college account each year without destroying other parts of the management plan. Each of the children have worked part-time, and other sources of financial assistance have been obtained to make up the difference. Each year we've been able to assume a larger portion of these expenses.

Increase giving for Christian ministries.—From the beginning we increased our percentage of giving through our church. This was accomplished in two ways. First, we set a goal to maintain the same amount of gifts after my wife resigned her job as while she was working. This increased our giving beyond the 10 percent we had maintained throughout the years. Second, we started budgeting mission gifts each month. This made it much easier to increase those gifts without jeopardizing our management plan in those months when the offerings were actually given.

Begin volunteer literacy mission work.—This was another part of our giving for Christian ministries but through more direct involvement. It mostly involved providing funds in our management plan for my wife's transportation. This included transporting a minimal number of the refugees (all she could get into a car) to central locations to attend literacy classes, to the grocery store, doctor, looking for housing, and to some of their homes for personal tutoring. Initially, this required only $40 per month for gasoline for a car. As the needs continued to grow we purchased a used, twelve-passenger van for transportation, but that proved to be too much for us to maintain. The level of involvement is back to car size for my wife, but other Christians and churches have now gotten more involved.

We accomplished all of the goals we set for that first year and more on what at first appeared to be a reduced income. There's no way to guarantee the same results for you, but even if different, yours can be just as rewarding. My enthusiasm for goal setting has been greatly increased these past years.

Goals for the Next Five Years

Pay cash for cars.—During the first two years of our management plan, we were unable to start saving money specifically for car replacement. We had two cars, four and five years old. Neither of them was very dependable because of high mileage. But we planned to drive them until we could trade without using credit. When one of the cars was totaled in an accident just over one-and-one-half years into our planning, a decision had to be made about replacement.

Should we continue with one car or use the small emergency fund to replace it? If we didn't replace it, my wife's literacy work would be curtailed, and that was a major motivation for our management planning. We decided to use the emergency money along with the insurance money received from the wrecked car but no more. (Money management makes these kinds of choices possible.) I found a three-year-old lease car which I could buy wholesale. After taxes and title, I had $7 left in the emergency fund. But I had paid cash for the car.

Since then, I have bought three other vehicles, including the van for literacy work, without using credit. Here's the plan I'm basically using.

It's based on a one-year plan repeated three times or more.

At least one year in advance of trading cars I begin to make payments on a car by putting the money into a savings account. At one point, the car I needed to trade was valued at about $1500. I estimated that to trade for a new car with credit would require monthly payments of just over $200. So I begin to save $200 per month for car replacement.

At the end of the first year, my $1500 car had depreciated to about $1300, but I had saved $2600 ($2400 plus $200 interest earned). Allowing for at least $200 extra repairs for the old car, at the end of the first year I had $3700 cash and trade-in to use for car replacement. (I had been able to save a little extra, so I purchased a $4500 car that first time.) The following outline indicates how the plan works over a three-year period. (Interest earned on savings is not included.)

Depreciated Car Value	Savings Per Year	Money & Trade-in Available
$1300	$2400	$3700
$3300	$2400	$5700
$5100	$2400	$7500

At the end of three years, there is a cash value of $7500 either in a car or a combination of car and money.

Now compare the difference if I had financed a $7500 new car at the beginning of the three-year period. (There are not many $7500 new cars around, but I don't buy new cars any way.) With my $1500 trade-in, I would have financed $6000. At 10 percent simple interest (if you can borrow money at that rate), I would have paid at least $1800 interest over the three-year period: a payback of $7800, $216.66 per month. Because of more rapid depreciation the first two years on a new car, at the end of three years my $7500 car would have been valued at about $5000. When the $1800 interest paid is subtracted from my $5000 car, my net value related to the car would be $3200.

Over the three-year period, if I used cash, I would have invested $8700 ($1500 original car value plus 3 × $2400 savings). Using credit, I would have invested $9300 ($1500 original car value plus $6000 financed plus $1800 interest). At first, that appears to amount to only $600 in savings. But look closer. Using the cash payment plan, I could have a new car at this point instead of a car three years old. That's worth at least $2500. Further, after the first year, the interest I would earn on my savings would not likely be used in extra repairs, another $400 gain.

The net savings by using cash instead of credit is $3500 over a three-year period ($600 less money invested, plus $2500 less depreciation, and $400 earned in interest). That's 40 percent savings. (If you stop the second year and drive a two-year-old car, as I do, the savings will be almost 70 percent. I can own two very dependable cars for less than what one new car would cost if bought on credit.)

Begin an investment program.—Now into the fifth year of our management plan, this is the only one of our one-to-five year goal not yet accomplished. However, some savings have been made each of the past two years and before the end of the current year I anticipate that this goal, too, will be achieved.

Participate in a special mission project.—When first set as one of our goals, the idea for a special mission project was rather nebulous. It was based more on desire than on a clear direction. However, it materialized in both the third and fourth years of our management plan. My wife has gone to Upper Volta, West Africa, three times (for four weeks each trip) to teach literacy. It's such a joy to see goals materialize and often grow in significance. What started as local literacy mission involvement developed into a foreign mission involvement. And it's continuing to grow through my wife's commitment to training literacy volunteers for local and foreign mission work.

Long-Range Goals

Pay off home mortgage.—As is true with some goals that extend twenty years or more, paying off our home mortgage may or may not be a wise thing to do. It depends on the economy and other factors. But behind the goal are plans to either pay off the mortgage or have investments which will make the payments for us by the time we retire. (The interest rate on our mortgage is much lower than current rates.)

If you should want to pay off your mortgage early, there is a simple method which can be used. You should have an amortization schedule for the length of your mortgage which shows the amount of principle and interest to be applied each month. If your mortgagee agrees, you can pay the exact principle of your next month's payment which will eliminate the total last payment on the schedule. For example, my present principle payment is about $39 per month. It increases a few cents each month and interest decreases by the same amount. If I paid the approximate $39 extra next month, I would eliminate the 360th payment of $346 shown on my amortization schedule. If I continued this method each month, the remaining twenty-five years of mortgage would be paid in twelve and one-half years. The extra principle paid will continue to increase each month, however, to over $150 by the end of the twelve and one-half years.

Other long-range goals.—We plan to continue and refine some kind of investment program once we get started this year. We are also planning for an extended mission project, maybe in retirement if our health permits. Now we are thinking in terms of a year or more in home or foreign mission work.

This review of the goals we set that first year reflect change and refinement with time. Obviously, several other short- and medium-range goals have been added in the past four years. Though goals may be planned at any time during the year, they are usually funded in our management plan once each year when we do "annual planning." Your goals will likely be different than ours, but I hope this review will suffice as a clear example of the kind of goals which can be chosen and accomplished. Such goal setting is a project in which the whole family should be involved, if you're married.

Estimating Your Income

Because of human nature, it is wise to choose your goals before estimating your income. When the order is reversed, we tend to limit our goals by the amount of our present income. This may seem logical since we should strive to live within our means, but it reduces the motivation to develop better management skills. If we never challenge our abilities, we'll never escape the present. William James, a famous psychologist, said, "Anything the mind can believe and conceive, it can achieve."[1] He may not have been completely right, but he wasn't completely wrong either.

Income is directly related to goal accomplishments and management, but it also has other connotations. It can be understood in at least three ways: perceived worth, potential for serving and helping, and buying power.

Income as Perceived Worth

It is nearly impossible to escape the economic influences of our society. Earning money, buying, and selling are a large part of our daily activities. The majority of life decisions are reduced to economics. (Observe your next social conversation with friends and see how much of it is influenced by economics.) Thus much of our casual decision making is based on cost/benefit analysis. In such a pervasively economic society, we are led to believe that self-worth is determined by our income.

This overemphasis on income as self-worth tends to reduce all goals to acquiring more money. We overwork and spend our money for more unsatisfying goods and services. Many of us are inflicted by the "mad child" syndrome which D. H. Lawrence wrote about in "The Rocking Horse Winner." The child "constantly heard voices in his family's house, saying, 'There must be more money! There must be more money!' The child raced himself to death on a rocking horse, just as we drive ourselves—never satisfied, never catching up with our desires."[2] Not only do we measure our own worth by our income, we measure the worth of others by their income.

A great tragedy occurs when self-worth based on income is applied to one's spouse. Tradition generally attributes this kind of thinking to a wife who wants to remain in the home and be provided for in luxury by her husband. If he fails to provide the standard of living she desires, she labels him a failure and inadequate as a spouse. (A typical soap opera plot.) But more than ever, husbands are relating to their wives in terms of the wife's ability to produce income for the family. In a report by the Population Reference Bureau based on the 1980 census, 50 percent of women over sixteen years of age are employed outside of the home. Of these, 70 percent are working out of a perceived necessity to help their households keep pace with inflation.

Many wives who are a part of the 70 percent category, if they knew they had a choice, likely would prefer not being employed. This is not meant to be a criticism of wives who want to be employed. Most working wives are making a worthwhile contribution to society and humanity as a whole. I'm very aware that adverse family circumstances have forced many wives to seek employment. Other wives choose to work for a time to help their husbands achieve career goals which may include education.

My wife prefers not to be employed at the present time in order to give more time to voluntary literacy mission work. Because of the contribution she's capable of making to Christian ministry, I've encouraged her to return to college to complete her degree. Upon graduation she may choose to be employed again as a means of fulfilling her calling. If so, it will be a voluntary choice, not a necessity.

It is to many of the 70 percent who would rather not be employed and who want to make their contribution in another way that I'm saying there may be an alternative. Many are laboring under a misconception about the amount of additional income they are actually producing. Their employment may even be costing them money rather than paying them. Look at a typical expense breakdown of a typical spouse. This illustration is based on a $7800 per year salary ($4 per hour, 37.5 hours per week).

$ 546 Income tax withholdings
$ 492 FICA (Social Security)
$ 51 Other withholdings (Insurance, etc.)
$ 720 Transportation (14 miles per day at 20 cents per mile)
$ 936 Giving at 12 percent (regular and mission giving)
$ 520 Extra clothes, cleaning, etc., because of employment
$2400 Additional cost for household operation ($200 per month is used here as the amount we were able to save on food, etc. when my wife began to plan menus, eliminate the use of prepared

and junk foods, and generally practice
household management.)

$ 780   "I-deserve-it-because-I'm-working"   money,
gifts at the office, etc. (10 percent of salary)

$1374   Increase in income tax ($1920 increase less $546
withheld)

$7819   TOTAL COST TO BE EMPLOYED

From this case study, the net benefit to the family as a
result of the wife's employment is a loss of $19. You will
note that I didn't include child care. If you think my $2400
for increased household operation is excessive, child care
services, if needed, would likely make up for the difference
and probably more. I also didn't include charges for parking.
Further, this example doesn't account for additional money
spent as the result of a perceived ability to enjoy a higher
standard of living. When the self-worth of a wife is measured by income produced and that income is subjected to
cost/benefit analysis, her worth may be negative. As Christians, we know that's not the way God created us or the
family.

Income as Potential

The previous discussion is not an attempt to discredit
earning money but a candid evaluation of a misconception.
Income can represent a part of a person's worth as it reflects
potential for helping and serving; God created us to be responsible in this way. He created us with the ability and
with the responsibility to work in order to provide for our
physical needs. The first example of human management
assignment involved work: "The Lord God took the man
and put him into the garden of Eden to cultivate it and keep
it" (Gen. 2:15). Throughout the Bible, honest work is the
basis for earning money to provide for one's support.

Deuteronomy 8:18 reminds us that it is God who gives us power to make wealth, and Paul wrote the Thessalonians not to be lazy, that "if anyone will not work, neither let him eat" (2 Thess. 3:10).

The first principle of work is to do it for God; "Whatever you do, do your work heartily, as for the Lord rather than for men; knowing that from the Lord you will receive the reward of the inheritance. It is the Lord Christ whom you serve" (Col. 3:23-24). A Christian employee, skilled in the work assigned, should be the best employee an employer could have on the job. When a Christian reports for work, the integrity of his or her commitment to Christ is on review. And according to Paul's instructions to Timothy, our Christian integrity is evident in the way we provide for our family (1 Tim. 5:8).

Income as potential is especially evident in the Christian work ethic. Scripture supports the right and responsibility to provide for oneself and family (1 Tim. 5:8). But unlike the secular ethic, providing for self and family is not the only reason for working to earn money. Our larger responsibility and potential include working to help others. "Let him who steals steal no longer; but rather let him labor, performing with his own hands what is good, in order that he may have something to share with him who has need" (Eph. 4:28). This is very basic to our relationship with God as fellow worker (1 Cor. 3:9). A non-Christian can be motivated to work by the fear of hunger, the responsibility to provide for his family, and even honest and worthwhile work. But a Christian has an additional and higher motive for working to earn money: to have something to share with people in need.

Income as Buying Power

The two previous views of income are somewhat philosophical/psychological and spiritual respectively. But in a workable money management plan, actual buying power needs to be determined, also. Whether you are a professional, self-employed person or a wage earner, the end result is the same. Before a "plan for spending" can be developed, gross income needs to be reduced to spendable income. This is the *second step* in developing a management plan.

Estimating your income (buying power) has a future orientation. It's looking ahead, an estimate of what you expect your income to be until some future date—an annual cost of living increase, increased production and sales, a merit increase or promotion. (Hopefully it won't be a decrease in income.) A spending plan is based on estimated income for the period of time until a change in income is expected.

This process is only slightly more difficult for professional, self-employed persons than for wage earners whose income is usually constant. Those whose income fluctuates can arrive at an average anticipated income and proceed as if it were the same each week or month.

First, arrive at an estimate of gross income. This will include salaries, self-employment income, interest and dividends, Social Security, pensions, income from hobbies, alimony, child support, and any other sources from which you may anticipate receiving money.

Second, reduce this amount by the amount of income tax and Social Security withholdings, and any other payroll deductions such as insurance and dues. (Self-employed persons who personally remit taxes to the Internal Revenue Service monthly or quarterly will probably want to include them in the spending plan [next chapter] rather than deduct-

ing them from gross earnings in this step. You have to manage your own tax payments rather than having an employer
manage them for you.) The results of this exercise reveal
your spendable income or buying power. In preparation for
developing a spending plan, it is usually best to reduce your
findings here to a "monthly" spendable income.

There are at least three possible advantages in working
through this step. It discourages any attempt to develop a
plan for spending on gross income. (I used to use my gross
income when trying to convince lenders to let me have more
credit.) Through this analysis of income, you may discover
a significant amount of incidental income which has been
"falling through the cracks" and making little or no contribution to your financial situation. Income from a hobby or
even interest income are examples. And it may help you to
be more grateful for God's provisions. (Note your fringe
benefits.)

If you tend to be a bit impatient, as I am, it may be difficult
to get excited about so much management planning—setting
goals, estimating income, and such. But planning is important and essential before getting to work on your spending
plan. As I understand it, planning is a part and not a prelude
to Christian money management. We all can likely benefit
from the wisdom of Ecclesiastes: "There is an appointed
time for everything. And there is a time for every event
under heaven" (3:1). Planning just happens to be one of
them.

Notes

1. Quoted by Venita VanCaspel, *The Power of Money Dynamics* (Reston, Virginia:
Reston Publishing Company, Inc., 1983), p. 5.

2. D. H. Lawrence, "The Rocking Horse Winner," *Exploring Literature Through Reading
and Writing,* eds. Bernard A. Drabeck, Helen E. Ellis, and Hartley A. Pfeil (Boston:
Houghton Mifflin Company, 1982), p. 730.

6
Management Applied: Spending and Records

The sincerity of Christians' commitment to Christian money management is exposed at the point of application. Many times prior to my pilgrimage in money management, I would write down my income and expenses with a resolve to manage my money better. After a week or two, I would lose track of my spending because of lack of commitment and abandon the whole plan. Actually, my finances were in worse shape after each such attempt than before. Psychologically, I perceived myself as being incapable of functioning any differently. With each failure, this accepted inability was more deeply ingrained.

Tom Parrish, a lawyer and retired development officer for Baylor University, Waco, Texas, says, "The way we perceive ourselves will determine how we act." Apply that thought to money management. Some of us may regularly make unwise spending decisions because we believe the knowledge necessary to make wise decisions is unobtainable. Thus we perceive ourselves as being at the mercy of knowledgeable merchandisers. We may perceive that culture has us locked in and that we can't change our life-style. Or we perceive that budgeting household expenses is impossible because life is too complex, too fast, and too changeable. Even worse is perceiving ourselves as unable to be good managers because of too many external pressures.

I'm reminded of a young friend who was about to graduate from high school. He was asked what he was going to do after graduation. Reflecting a moment he responded, "I guess I'll start to college and then drop out like many others I know." Had that been a serious perception, that's probably what he would have done. "The way we perceive ourselves determines how we act." My wife tells me that a major part of teaching illiterates to read and write is helping them to perceive themselves differently. As long as a person thinks he's a failure, he will be one. As long as you think you can't change your management patterns, you won't change them.

God created you a manager! It's right to perceive yourself as being just that. However, God created you with the ability; it's up to you to get the facts and learn how to apply the biblical principles of management to daily living. So you may need to work on both perception and obtaining additional information.

The *third step* in developing your management plan, determining past spending, should help you gather some of the needed information. It's not enough to be able to make money; you need to know how you're spending it. It has long been recognized that there are many people in the upper income bracket who lack management skills. A low management perception is not limited to low income families. In fact, many low income families are excellent managers.

Determine Past Spending

Like estimating your income, determining past spending habits is another building block for developing a spending plan. There is nothing technical or mysterious about this process. However, it will require some discipline and time on your part. If this is accepted as a part of your commitment to Christian money management, it can be rewarding and much less tedious.

Your spending can be divided into at least two categories —fixed expenses and flexible expenses. The "Expenses/Plan for Spending" chart on page 120 lists thirty-eight items to help you remember the kinds of things for which you spend money. Items 1 to 14 reflect typical fixed expenses and items 15 to 38 are typical flexible expenses. Ignore those items which do not apply to you and add items unique to your spending habits.

Fixed Expenses

Fixed expenses may be divided into monthly and irregular expenses. Study the first fourteen items of the chart. For example, for those of us still making them, home mortgage (rent) payments are normally a fixed, monthly amount. The monthly amount for mortgage payments and all other regular monthly payments can be determined and, if you wish, recorded in the "Monthly Average Expenses Last Year" column beside the appropriate item.

Other fixed expenses are irregular. Items such as home insurance, taxes, and life and automobile insurance may be paid in three, six, or twelve month installments but in the same amount each time. These items can be reduced to a monthly amount and recorded as fixed monthly expenses.

The "loan payment" item is for a major loan other than a home mortgage. This might be a bank loan for a car or home improvements. The "total other debts" item would be for the combined total monthly payments on revolving charge purchases. The item is placed here in fixed expenses for those who particularly want to eliminate the practice of charging routine expenses and want to pay off all existing charges. When a plan for spending is developed, items charged should be planned for in the appropriate item ac-

count. If clothing is charged, it would then be deducted from
the clothing item account. Thus the "total other debts" item
would not normally be used.

Items such as income tax and Social Security which are
remitted by an employer would be omitted. These items are
placed on the form for the benefit of professional/self-employed persons who normally remit their own taxes to the
Internal Revenue Service.

Flexible Expenses

Your flexible expenses vary from one month to another.
Examples of these expenses are food, utilities, automobile,
clothing, and medical costs. Items 15 to 38 on the "Expenses/Plan for Spending" chart will help you remember
many of these items. To determine your flexible expenses
for the past year will probably require more research than
for fixed expenses. The resources which will help provide
this information are checkbook ledgers, utility bill stubs,
and various other receipts from visits to the doctor and
dentist, prescription drugs, automobile repairs, and so forth.

You may want to list items 15 to 38 on the left side of a
sheet of paper. Across the top of the page, list the previous
twelve months of the year. On the right side of the page
leave room for a column labeled "Average Monthly Expenses." As receipts are available, record the amount for the
appropriate item under the month in which it occurred. This
exercise will reveal that many of the flexible expenses are
somewhat constant, others are seasonal, and some are unpredictable. The objective of this step is to arrive at a reasonably accurate monthly average expense for each item.

A caution and a tip may be helpful at this point. The
caution is that this can be a particularly discouraging exercise. Unless you are among the small percentage of people
who normally keep accurate records, you will have many

blank spaces on your paper after you've recorded the most obvious expenses. I'm writing from experience. It may take unusual determination to continue. Please do! I can guarantee that the benefits later on will greatly outweigh the depression at this point.

Now the tip. When looking over your checkbook ledger, there will likely be checks written for "cash" and other unremembered expenditures. You may not have the records to show where you've been spending much of your money, but you may be surprised at how much you already know about your spending. Try pondering your grocery expenses. My guess is that you will almost instinctively know about how much you're spending. Proceed in this same fashion with each item for which you don't have receipts. Make educated guesses but be realistic. There's probably no need to try to estimate for each month; just guess at a monthly average and record it in the last column. This is how I got started.

After completing this step, total all fixed and flexible monthly average expenses. This total becomes an important figure as you continue to develop your management plan.

Developing a Plan for Spending

Developing your plan for spending is the *fourth step* in your management plan. Each step I've discussed builds on the previous one. Let's review them briefly.

Step one is choosing your goals (chapter 5). This step builds on the biblical basis for Christian money management. Obviously, the entire management plan should be justified by biblical teachings. But since goals reflect our understanding of our purpose for living, they become the first expression of our commitment.

Step two is estimating your income (chapter 5). The objective of

EXPENSES / PLAN FOR SPENDING[1]

ACCOUNT ITEM	Monthly Average Exps. Last Yr.	Monthly Plan for Spending	Income Allocations			
			1	2	3	4
1. Church gifts	$	$	$	$	$	$
2. Home mortgage						
3. Home insurance						
4. Home taxes						
5. Savings & emergency						
6. Income taxes						
7. Social Security						
8. Retirement						
9. Life insurance						
10. Health & accident insurance						
11. Hospital insurance						
12. Auto insurance						
13. Loan payment						
14. Total other debts						
15. Food						
16. Clothing						
17. Gas						
18. Electricity						
19. Water						
20. Telephone						
21. Home improvements						
22. Home furnishings						
23. Home maintenance						
24. Auto repair						
25. Auto gasoline & oil						
26. Auto license						
27. Medical & dental						
28. Drugs						
29. Hospital						
30. Subscriptions						
31. School expenses						
32. Cleaning, laundry						
33. Allowances						
34. Toiletries, cosmetics						
35. Recreation, vacation						
36. Gifts, birthday, weddings						
37. Christmas						
38. Other						
39.						
40.						
TOTAL		$	XXXXXXXXXXXXXXXXXXXXXXXXXX			
TOTAL EACH INCOME ALLOCATION			$	$	$	$

this step was to arrive at a monthly spendable income. It looks forward to the next anticipated change in income, usually within the next twelve months. This means it is present income unless the management plan is being prepared in advance of an anticipated increase or decrease. This would be the situation if you have been using a management plan and are about to redesign it to accommodate a changing income which is imminent.

Step three is determining past spending. This step looked back to the previous twelve months. It is important to note that income is projected forward and expenses are for the previous year. This difference will need to be allowed for when your plan for spending is being written. Increased costs, which should include some inflation, will need to be planned for.

Comparing Income and Spending

Step four begins with a comparison of income and expenses. Simply subtract "average monthly expenses" determined in step three from "average estimated income" projected in step two. The balance may be positive or negative. If there is more income than expenses, that's great. But read on. The following discussion may help you discover even more surplus money. If your balance is negative, don't quit now. I'm going to discuss some possible solutions.

PRINCIPLE FOUR: **Our attitude influences our money management.**

Attitude.—I'm familiar with negative balances from past years, and I've found a solution that has worked for me. A major part of the solution was a change in attitude. Consider a basic question: Why are your expenses more than income? The first temptation is to blame it on not enough income.

That was the major fallacy in my attitude for years. I believed the solution to all financial problems was more money. I used to dream of "coming into a lot of money" in some mysterious way. But more money is seldom the solution. I've read that the majority of people who inherit or otherwise acquire large sums of money, if they have financial problems at the time, will be financially destitute again within a short time. From observation, I have no reason to doubt that conclusion.

A possible solution to more outgo than income or how to discover more surplus money may be a change in attitude about money. Secular society has taught us that more is better, and more money is the solution to most financial problems. Our Christian faith counsels us otherwise. But we often let secular attitudes mold our thinking. We jokingly say, "Money may not buy happiness, but it buys the kind of misery we enjoy." Just making the statement in a casual conservation may reveal a basic attitude about money.

Attitudes about money are sometimes developed by a single experience in our lives, often during our childhood. When at this point in developing my own management plan, an evaluation of my attitude toward money surfaced a fourth grade incident which had shaped my attitude for over thirty years. It involved my childhood sweetheart who was enticed to "dump" me for another boy. Though I'm aware now that the boy's family probably had no more money than mine, he was allowed much more spending money than I. He stole my sweetheart with chewing gum and candy. I didn't have the money with which to counter his advances.

I'm rather sure that this isolated, childhood experience caused me to place too much emphasis on the importance of money. Having money was equated with power over other people, influencing circumstances for personal advantage, and getting what I wanted when I wanted it. Since childhood romances are some of the most memorable experiences in life, their relationship to the use of money could shape lifelong attitudes.

Your childhood romances may have nothing to do with your attitude about money. What I want to suggest, however, is that you reflect upon the experiences in your life which have shaped your attitude in the use of money. Ask yourself how your parents or significant adults in your life used money? What impressions do you recall about allowances or your first job? What have been your dreams about money throughout life? Evaluate particularly how you feel about power, influence, and pleasure as they relate to money. Since evaluations, of necessity, must be one thing compared to another, use the biblical management assignment and your purpose in life to image God as your standard. You may find it helpful to record some of your reflections.

An evaluation of your attitude about money may reveal why you do or don't do certain things. For example, I'm rather sure that my abuse of credit was related to some degree to my attitude about money developed in the fourth grade. The ability to purchase things for myself and my family proved that I was just as "good" as that boy who stole my girl friend. The fact that I had to use credit to impress myself and others was immaterial. With the support society gave me in this direction, it didn't take long to lose control.

PRINCIPLE FIVE: **A commitment to biblical management prevents mismanagement.**

Reduce Upkeep.—Another possible solution for balancing your income and spending (or freeing more money) is to reduce your upkeep. Though attitude about money influences all of us to some degree, there may be a very tangible solution. Thoreau wrote in *Walden* that "We live pushing all of our things before us."[2] Everything we own demands an expenditure of our time, energy, and money. Most things either have to be cleaned, painted, warmed, cooled, greased, repaired, or all of the above.

In looking for a way to reduce expenses, consider what you own and what contribution these things are making to your family unity, Christian witness, and livelihood. Look at your fixed expenses; are you still paying for some of the things that are creating more of a drain than a contribution? If something is making a worthwhile contribution, could a smaller one (house) or a less expensive model (car) provide a similar benefit? If you discover something that is seldom used (bass boat), consider selling it and renting the item when it's needed. Your investment could be freed for more worthwhile purposes.

Adjust Spending Habits.—Consider your flexible expenses. Adjustments in the food category reduced my family's expenses by the largest amount, about $200 per month. Four adjustments made this possible. First and most significant was planning menus. My wife has encouraged me to emphasize the value of planning menus when writing about money management and when leading conferences. It may seem tedious at first if you have resisted this sort of thing, but it gets easier. After six or eight weeks for most families, the menus can be repeated with slight variations to accommodate sale items. An added plus is not having to consume time each day thinking about what to prepare for meals.

The second adjustment is related to the first; reduce the number of convenience foods purchased. Prepared foods cost more and are usually less tasty. When meals improve as they did at our house, it's hard to think of careful money management as somehow being a sacrifice.

The third adjustment was to reduce the amount of "junk food" purchases. As soft drinks, chips, and other items were reduced over a period of time, we've reached the point now to where they are seldom purchased but without feeling we've given up anything. They do still appear on special occasions.

The fourth adjustment to food expenditures was to limit the number of trips to the grocery store. This relates to the first three adjustments. Planning menus and purchasing groceries for two week periods reduced the number of shopping trips. Thus the temptation to buy food impulsively was curtailed. The next time you visit a grocery store, notice where the milk, bread, and meat are located. They will be at the most distant point from the entrance. The traffic flow is designed to take you past the junk foods first.

Continue to examine other flexible expenses which might help you balance income and expenses. Clothing expenses may be reduced. Unless you can make your own clothes, the next best thing is to purchase clothes on sale or find wholesale outlets. We use both of these methods effectively. I've also discovered another neat idea; it's mixing and matching. When preparing for a change in season, separate all existing clothing into categories—pants, shirts, blouses, coats, blazers, ties, scarves, belts, shoes, purses, and so on. Determine what will match for different looking outfits and what separate items could be purchased to coordinate existing items. Such coordination will often yield additional new outfits inexpensively.

When management becomes a way of life, you will discover other ways to adjust your spending habits. Expenses for utilities can be reduced by most all families with some conscious effort. This is possible even when there are teenagers in the home who stay in the shower thirty minutes twice each day, who appear to be completely unaware of the "off" function of light switches, and who can always think of someone to call long distance. I've noted already how retrofitting the house—weather stripping, caulking, and insulating—has produced beneficial results for me with minimum expenditure of money. You might also consider getting a calling card if you make several personal long-distance calls away from your home telephone, such as children in college calling home collect. Or one of the alternate long-distance telephone services can save you as much as 25 percent on daytime calls and 10 percent at night.

Credit Abuse.—I continue to refer to the use and misuse of credit because of the problems it has caused and continues to cause for so many people. I'm convinced that it can be a major cause of mismanagement, even when all charge purchases are paid in full each month. The credit card companies themselves acknowledge that people who habitually charge routine purchases will spend about 20 percent more than people who pay cash. The reason is psychological. It is psychologically easier to hand over a piece of plastic than it is to part with cash. It is also somewhat easier to write a check than it is to pay with cash.

Charles Wesley Shike, a priest of the Episcopal Church and practicing psychoanalyst, has identified a "debt proneness" in some people.[3] He first notes "a desire to maintain a childlike relationship to authority." An indebtedness to a bank, for example, is similar to a time of dependence on one's parents. Such a dependency need exists to some degree in all of us. But Shike notes that it is pronounced in alcoholics, overeaters, gamblers, and those who are debt prone.

Second, Shike has determined that

> many people crave a sense of obligation. . . . The American culture sometimes resembles, in its credit system, the old company store . . . where supplies were always available, at

the price of obligation. . . . In this sense, the 'affluent poor,' who may have nice homes and drive nice cars, become participants in the welfare state and have feelings similar to people on welfare.

Based on a fear of independence and autonomy, the debtor is trapped by creditors who promise to provide them security, often resulting in overextended credit. Then a reverse kind of security is derived by the debtor through obligation when the creditor demands payment.

The third aspect in "the debt prone person is the flight from pleasure." With the use of credit, a person can walk with millionaires for a brief time in sheer pleasure. Then when the bills start to come and creditors harrass him, the person's low estimate of his self-worth is reinforced. This is a masochistic response. "For the masochist, all pleasure must be paid for with an equal or greater amount of suffering or punishment." When the punishment has run its course— bankruptcy or other penalties—the debtor usually begins the cycle over again. Too often this is the contribution which the great American way of credit makes to people's lives. Some marriage counselors estimate that financial problems, many of which involve credit abuse, are a root cause in 75 percent of marital conflicts.[4]

The use of credit is habit-forming. Reflecting upon my own past experiences of credit abuse and observing people close to me, I can see a definite pattern. First, there is experiment. Caught without cash, one purchase—often impulsive —is made with credit. Payment is made promptly with no ill effects. Second, planning ahead for purchases is relaxed, and the need to use credit becomes easier to justify. Third, as obligations for repayment of debts increase, most all planning ahead is abandoned and the focus is backward. An increasing amount of thought, energy, and resources must be devoted to managing the debt(s) and enlarging debt limits. The addiction is complete. Getting off of the credit merry-go-round without getting crushed is nearly impossible.

Since the use of credit is so common, I would encourage you to carefully evaluate your use of it if you do use credit regularly. You could be far from financial trouble and still be mismanaging your resources because of dependence on the credit system. Wise use of credit or restricting its use could greatly improve your management and cash flow.

Wise use of credit.—There are some areas where credit can be used wisely and to your advantage. Obviously, if a member of my family needed emergency medical help and credit was my only recourse, I would use it. Generally, I have no problem with using credit cards when traveling, particularly if it's business travel where receipts and reports are required. I consistently use a credit card for my business travel for records and safety.

Another area of credit which can be used with wisdom is the home mortgage and the establishment of a business. As long as the economy is reasonably stable and the amount borrowed is secured with equal assets, this is considered more of an investment than credit. Secured loans to attend college would normally be in this category. But in this there are limits, and wisdom and discretion should be used. Keep in mind that debt is created when something that depreciates is purchased on the credit system. If an item which appreciates is purchased with credit, it's an investment.

At the heart of all of the solutions I've proposed to balance income and expenses or to create more surplus money is the need for planning. The single greatest cause of mismanagement is the lack of planning.

PRINCIPLE SIX: **Christian management guides our use of money and material things.**

Recording Your Plan for Spending

When anticipated income and estimated expenses have been reconciled, hopefully with some amount of surplus money, *step four,* "Make a Plan for Spending," is completed by recording proposed spending. This is your working budget from the present until the next expected change in income. There is a column on the "Expenses/Plan for Spending" chart for this purpose. It's the column headed "Monthly Plan for Spending."

The dollar amounts for each item in the "Monthly Average Expenses Last Year" column can be increased using any surplus money available when you compare income and expenses. Increases should be based on real need. As a Christian manager, choose your life-style intentionally. It is not necessary to raise your standard of living to the limit of your income. Some items will necessarily need to be increased, often because of inflation. Others such as gifts through your church can be increased by choice. This is the time to be guided by your goals established in *step one.* But don't give up if you can't have a perfect budget the first try. The first year we didn't have enough money for a miscellaneous item or for gifts. But when other areas of spending are being managed, you can compensate for an imperfect budget.

If you're married, developing your plan for spending should definitely include your spouse and children who are old enough to understand and participate. Involvement of the whole family throughout the entire process is encouraged because at this point their use of money is going to be determined. They need to know and understand the reason for having a management plan.

A special note for professional/self-employed persons is in order at this point. Your income will likely vary each month. If you have arrived at a reasonably accurate average monthly income—*step two*—develop your plan for spending using that amount. In addition, include an item in your plan labeled "reserve fund" or whatever name you might want to call it. For the months when your income exceeds the average, apply the overage to the "reserve fund." Then in months when income is less than the average budgeted, draw from the "reserve fund" to achieve the average.

The chart on page 120 also has four columns labeled "Income Allocations." If income received is more frequent than once per month or if both spouses have income, these columns can be used to apply the sources of income to the item accounts. For example, if a person has two income periods per month in the same amount each time, two columns can be used. Half of the monthly requirement for each item account can be funded each income period. If there are two sources of income, they can be combined and treated as one. Some item accounts can be funded each month by one income source and the remaining item accounts funded by the other income.

Keep Simple, Accurate Records

There is a great difference in keeping financial records and in managing finances. Effective money management requires that a person be familiar with ongoing expenses in various categories in order to control expenses for individual items. For example, management is not effective when a spouse issues a general edict that family expenses must be reduced immediately by all members. What does that mean? Walking to work and school instead of driving? Eating beans and corn bread? Going to bed at sunset to save electricity? For how long? No one in the family will know what it means except the one giving the edict. If, however, the family were to be informed on the twentieth day of the month that the clothing budget was used up, that would be understood. Family members would know not to make further clothing purchases until the first of the next month, a ten-day wait.

Developing a Simple Record System

The record system is *step five* of the management plan. In developing your plan for spending (budget), a portion of your income was allocated to each item you anticipate needing to spend money for in the near future. To ensure that the portion of your income assigned to each item will be available when expenses occur, a system is needed to keep track of items individually. An example "Item Account" form is provided on page 133. This is simply a suggested form. Other types can be purchased or you can design your own. Whatever form you may choose, the principle is the same and the illustrations used here will apply.

The likelihood of a budget being used is directly related to its simplicity. For this reason, the thirty-eight items on your plan for spending (more or less depending on your personalized version) may need to be combined into fourteen to twenty categories for record-keeping purposes.

On your plan for spending, you may have four different kinds of utilities—electricity, natural gas, telephone, and water. From the previous year's expenses, you determined what each utility cost. For example, electricity cost $1080 for the previous twelve months, an average of $90 per month. When developing your budget for the coming year (or until your next anticipated change in income), you allocated $95.50 per month for electricity because of expected rate increases.

Having used the same method to determine costs for each utility item, your anticipated costs for utilities per month might look something like this: electricity-$95.50; natural gas-$25; telephone-$35; water-$28. For record-keeping purposes, all four utility items can be combined into one utility item of $183.50 per month. When each of the four bills are paid for a month, all four would be deducted from the one utilities item account form. In fact, since the home mortgage (rent) payment is a fixed amount, it too could be included on this same item account form. However, I suggest that house upkeep not be included with utilities because maintenance is so variable.

Logical combinations of item accounts for a working household budget might look like this:

1. Church/Mission Gifts
2. Home Mortgage/Utilities
3. Savings/Emergency Fund/ Retirement
4. Insurance
5. Loans
6. Food/Toiletries
7. Clothing
8. Medical Expenses
9. Automobiles
10. House Upkeep
11. Children
12. Recreation/ Vacation
13. Gifts/Christmas
14. Miscellaneous

After combining the item accounts you choose, transfer the appropriate item account expenses and income allocations information for a month to separate item account forms. You may have fourteen to twenty different forms. I use twenty different item account forms. It is helpful to me to have two forms labeled "extra." I use these when money is received from a source that does not need to be combined with any other item. For instance, one of the children wants me to hold some money for a short time. I can deposit it in my bank account and keep it separated from my money by using one of the extra item account forms. I have made copies of the form found on page 133 and placed them in a three-ring notebook binder.

ITEM ACCOUNT[5]

Item Account Name _____ Monthly Plan for Spending $ _____

Income Allocation $_____ Income Allocation $_____ Income Allocation $_____ Income Allocation $_____

Check #	Date	Item Transactions	Deposits	With-drawals	Balance
Balance Forward from Previous Page					

Transfer last figure in balance column to next page.
(This is a sample form. Make your own form for each account. More than one form will be needed for some item accounts each year.)

Using the Record System

The development of a perfect budget and record system does not ensure successful money management. Regular use is required.

One checking account can be divided on paper into the fourteen to twenty item accounts illustrated. When income is received, it can be deposited into the checking account and recorded in the checkbook. Then the income is divided into the predetermined amounts and recorded on each item account form. Each item account form has a column to record deposits each income period. As expenditures occur for various items, the expenses are recorded in the withdrawals column. Another column reflects the accumulated balance for the item account after each deposit or expenditure.

This record system is kept up-to-date by transferring information from the checkbook. Each item account form functions like a "mini" checking account. It is easier to maintain accuracy when checks are used for most purchases. When cash is used, more extra note keeping is required. In our record system, I have one account from which I draw cash for pocket money. This item account is for my gasoline, lunches, and some miscellaneous expenses. I make note of expenses for which I use cash only if the expenditure is for something not related to my gasoline, lunches, and so forth. On the average, I find it necessary to make note of only two or three items each week. Since my wife mostly uses checks, she seldom if ever has to make extra notes of expenses.

For effective management, the records should be kept current at least weekly. When an accurate balance is reflected each week on the item account forms, decisions to reduce spending for individual items can be made before the budgeted amount is exceeded. This reflects a true management concept rather than just keeping a record of expenses. I find that keeping our records current requires fifteen minutes or so each week. This does not include the normal time used for paying bills and balancing the checkbook.

Up-to-date records are the basis for making all spending decisions, not the checkbook balance. If a clothing item needs to be purchased, check the balance on the clothing item account form before making your spending decision. After continued use, the whole process becomes nearly automatic. That's when you know that money management has become a part of your life-style. Encourage your children to become familiar with and refer to these records. They will learn to make their own responsible spending decisions. This makes a good contribution to harmony in the home.

Since average monthly expenses are projected for each item account and this amount is deposited to the item accounts each income period, surpluses should accumulate in some of the flexible item accounts. Utilities, for example, should accumulate some surplus during the spring and fall of the year. This accumulation will be there for the higher winter and summer utility bills.

Another example is automobile expenses. You may not need automobile repairs for an extended period of time. A $300 or $400 surplus may accumulate in this account. But don't spend it for something else. This is why spending decisions should never be based on the checkbook balance. The money in the bank is earmarked for something specific. What should you do with these surplus accumulations?

Before banks introduced NOW and SUPER NOW accounts, I suggested that account surpluses be transferred to passbook savings. This required a savings account form where each item account in savings could be kept separate. The transfer is no longer necessary if you convert your checking account to a NOW or SUPER NOW account. Not only can you earn interest on the account surpluses, but on all the money you have in your checking account. And this is possible without altering your basic record-keeping system. By converting my checking account to a SUPER NOW account, I'm earning about $200 per year interest. That $200 earned requires no thought, energy, or additional investment.

However, when money allocated specifically for savings or retirement accumulates sufficiently, such funds need to be placed in a higher interest yielding investment. For this kind of investment you may need or want to get some professional guidance. I do suggest that records be kept on the different kinds of savings. For example, the "Item Account" form can be used for each purpose for which savings are being accumulated—one form for an emergency fund, one for automobile replacement, and another for longer term investments. All of the savings may be in the same account but divided into item accounts the same as the checking account. You might come up with an even better idea.

Notes

1. Adapted from "Christian Family Money Management," a workbook (FS-1) published by the SBC Stewardship Commission, Nashville, Tennessee, April 1981, p. 12.

2. Henry David Thoreau, *Walden and Other Writings*, ed. Brooks Atkinson (New York: The Modern Library, 1937), p. 5.

3. Charles Wesley Shike, "The Psychological Reasons For Being 'Debt Prone,' " *Pastoral Aids #2*, (Lebanon, New Jersey: CRW Management Services, c. 1981).

4. Ed Hale, Lecture before the Educational Designs for Family Dynamics and Financial Planning Seminar, Lake Sharron Assembly, Lewisville, Texas, January 9-11, 1978. Mr. Hale is executive director, Dallas Teachers' Credit Bureau.

5. Adapted from "Christian Family Money Management" workbook, p. 15.

7
Management for the Future

After becoming familiar with the basic skills of money management, the task of planning for the future is still a large subject to grasp. My purpose in this chapter is to review the major elements involved. If after reading this chapter you are more aware of your Christian responsibility in this area, I will have accomplished my goal.

PRINCIPLE SEVEN: **Adhering to the biblical management doctrine balances responsibility of planning for the future with present responsibility for Christian ministries and family needs.**

A Christian Responsibility

Management for the future should not be thought of only in terms of the future. It is difficult, if not impossible, to separate the future from the present. It is like trying to separate salvation *now* from salvation *finally*. What happens now determines what will happen then. Though each stage of the family's or individual's life cycle will dictate a slightly different approach, planning for the future begins now with benefits growing in succeeding years. Wherever you are in the life cycle, planning for the future cannot be retroactive. Present management is required. If you use wisely the opportunity to plan for the future, time in retirement can be more enjoyable and meaningful because of not having to worry about financial survival.

Thinking about future financial needs creates tension for some Christians. For example, how does planning and saving for retirement reflect upon your Christian faith? After all, Jesus taught that we should not worry about tomorrow? Matthew 6:19-34, a part of Jesus' Sermon on the Mount, is a pointed discussion about not laying up wealth on earth. Rather, Jesus taught that our wealth should be stored in heaven, and with the promise that "all these things shall be added to you" (v. 33).

It is difficult to find New Testament texts which support planning for the future in such specific areas as insurance, savings, making a will, and retirement. The Scriptures which are used to support such planning are made to fit; they are often taken out of context. This does not mean, however, that there are no principles which can be applied.

To illustrate some of the difficulty I refer to, look at one of the Scripture passages sometimes used as a proof text. One Scripture used is Luke 12:20. The larger text of which this verse is a part is a parable on covetousness. It is about the man who had to build larger barns to accommodate an abundant harvest. But in Jesus' parable, he dies that very night and the question is asked: "Now who will own what you have prepared?" The question is timely; it is altogether appropriate when emphasizing the need for a Christian will for instance. But the Scripture was not written to encourage Christians to make wills; it was written to illustrate the absurdity of covetousness which leads to the improper use of wealth. (Other Scriptures sometimes used in this way include Matthew 25:14 *ff.*, Hebrews 11:4, and Revelation 14:13.)

Why are the Scriptures so silent on the subject of planning for the future if it is important for Christians? God's design for the family and management is probably the best clue we have. During Jesus' teaching ministry and before, this kind of planning was a design of the family structure. Jesus taught, "If a man says to his father or his mother, anything of mine you might have been helped by is Corban (that is to say, given to God), you no longer permit him to do anything for his father or his mother; thus invalidating the word of God by your tradition" (Mark 7:11-13). Committing all of one's resources to special "religious" uses was condemned by Jesus if it meant neglecting one's parents. Family members were to care for each other.

For example, there was no question as to where the father and mother would live in their old age. The oldest son inherited his father's estate and was responsible to provide for his parents. In fact, they had likely been living as a family clan all the while. This pattern continues to be used in many countries of the world. It is a natural design for mutual support. Other customs in the early Judeo-Christian culture provided for the care of family members when a husband and father died. It was essentially a closed system of planning for the eventual support of all family members. They did not have to concern themselves with complex inheritance laws and estate taxes.

Where does this leave planning for the future for Christians today? It leaves us with scriptural principles of management which will work in any culture and economic system. A major part of the management assignment God has given to us is responsibility for the material things with which he surrounds us. The prospect of dying does not alleviate that responsibility. In light of God's management design, it is irresponsible for a Christian to die and leave lifelong estate accumulation to be dissipated without purpose. Positively, consider the opportunity to use your estate to help enlarge God's kingdom and benefit others as a privilege and source of joy. Planning for the future should be viewed as the crowning touch to a Christian life.

The various subjects discussed in this chapter are all related to estate planning. But two of them are especially important for daily living and management decisions. For that reason, I've placed savings and insurance before the larger discussion of estate planning to emphasize their immediate importance.

Savings

Some Christians use their "faith" to justify a lack of wise planning for the future. You likely have heard many times that "faith is enough, and only faith will do." It is true that faith in Christ is extremely important for living and dying. But proper faith does not produce irresponsibility. To live up to your last dollar all of your life when it is unnecessary and die leaving only an empty shell of an estate to a dependent spouse or children is irresponsible. (See 1 Tim. 5:8.) Some even live in such reckless abandon that they not only leave no assets, they leave liabilities which create greater hardships for their survivors.

But there is another good reason I see for Christians to save: to ensure a continuing useful Christian life and accomplish significant goals. Without savings for emergencies, for example, a minor financial crisis could completely eliminate your ability to live an active Christian life for a period of time. It may even require other people to use their resources to help you and prevent them from being active in some good work they had planned. Saving for such things as your children's education and other important goals enriches life generally.

Saving for retirement is for much the same reason. When adequate retirement funds have not been planned for, very active and capable Christians often cannot continue their Christian involvement simply because they cannot afford to do so. This has been the situation I have observed when a pastor.

My convictions about Christians saving for emergencies and for retirement cannot be proof texted in the New Testament. Proverbs is about the only Scripture in the Bible where savings are encouraged. But the culture we have inherited makes savings now for a later time a Christian responsibility. Families are fragmented and mobile; we seldom live in family clans any more. In fact, those who do are looked upon as the unusual ones.

Savings for emergencies for most families should probably be equal to three months' salary. There are two reasons for this suggestion. The savings for emergencies should be very liquid; it should not be tied up in a way that would take several days or weeks to get your hands on it. The very nature of its purpose dictates this arrangement. Second, it seems unwise to have more than this amount of money uninvested in ways that would produce higher dividends. And having more than three months' wages available in easily accessible savings accounts may just be too great a temptation for many of us to keep from using the savings for some luxuries which we are able to justify.

Concerning savings and all planning for the future, I agree with VanCaspel.

If you prepare yourself and develop a spirit of serendipity, opportunity will always present itself. Don't just sit idly and say, 'God will provide.' God gave you talents, a mind, energy, and a strong body. You have all the tools you need to spade the productive loam, but God will not take your spade in hand. Don't sit and say 'The government will provide.' The government's efforts to provide are what have brought destructive inflation and higher and higher taxation.[1]

From the beginning, it was never intended that Social Security would be adequate for a person's retirement needs. But more and more Americans are depending on government for financial security in retirement. In 1969, 50 percent of Americans felt that retirement income was the responsibility of the individual. In 1979, only 30 percent believed it was their responsibility.[2]

Insurance

The most valuable asset you have is your life. Consider what it is worth to God and your family. Everything you do revolves around your life. If your life ceases, all that revolved around it begins to revolve around the lives of others. Death cancels our most valuable asset. The second best thing you can do for your family who depend on you for a supportive income is to provide life insurance. Life insurance, for the most part, is like the funeral; it is for the living.

The younger the family, the greater the need for life insurance. Most young families begin with a meager estate; life insurance creates an immediate death estate. Since the greatest amount of coverage is needed when most families are the least able to afford it, great care should be exercised when purchasing insurance. Thanks to the high interest returns on investments in the early 1980s, many policy holders with whole life coverage withdrew the cash value to invest the money at a higher interest rate. Insurance companies are now offering more flexible coverage which has resulted in better protection less expensively for many people.

Life Insurance as a Foundation

Often, life insurance is the foundation upon which all financial planning begins. As noted, this would be especially true for young families. Life insurance may be used to make more secure various kinds of real and personal property, but in broad terms the purpose for having it is twofold. First, the proceeds help bridge the gap between the income your heirs will have and what they will need. Namely, it is security for your family in the event of death. Second, it is to pay estate costs and/or preserve your estate. Of course, this relates very closely to the first, but it also goes beyond it.

Life insurance, to some extent, provides the insured with more peace of mind while fulfilling routine work assignments. For example, travel related to my work subjects me to greater risk to my life. But such reasonable risks usually increase the satisfaction and joy of living. In fact, without some risks life becomes purposeless and an attitude develops that makes life seem not really worth living. My life insurance helps prevent anxiety about my family's well-being if I should die or be killed.

Kinds of Insurance

There are basically three kinds of life insurance: whole or straight life with its many variations, term, and universal life. Whole life provides protection and cash value. Its premiums are the same from the age acquired throughout life or until the person reaches an age designated by the policy. Also, cash loans may be made against it or the policy may be surrendered for cash. But life insurance is an expensive way to achieve nondeath protection goals, say for retirement.

Term life insurance is the least expensive kind when used carefully throughout a person's lifetime. Premium rates are less expensive for younger people because only protection is being purchased. As a person becomes older, the rates increase. After age sixty-five, the rates become comparable with whole life insurance if purchased at the same age. The great advantage of term insurance is the fact that young families can more likely afford to provide adequate protection within their family budget. After children mature and establish their own homes, the amount of coverage can be decreased because the family estate has likely increased over the years. But this will vary from family to family. The presence of a handicapped child or invalid parents, for example, creates a unique situation which influences the kind and amount of insurance needed.

Universal life is a relatively new type of coverage that was introduced in the late 1970s and early 1980s. It is an insurance contract with life insurance protection and a cash account which earns current interest rates. The cash account is usually a money market-type fund. The uniqueness of this coverage is its flexibility. The face value of the life insurance can be changed without rewriting the policy. This allows the insured to lower or raise the premiums as family income varies. Also, the amount of the premium which is being placed in the high yielding money market fund can be varied. This type coverage has definite advantages over pure whole life policies, but there are some drawbacks. There are usually initial fees which must be paid when the policy is bought, and the part of the premiums which go into savings may earn less interest than if the individual invested and managed the fund personally.

Essentially, purchasing whole or universal life insurance is paying an insurance company to do your management for you which you can do better for yourself with a little investment of time. As a Christian manager, the wisest approach to insurance is to buy protection first. Cash values for savings can usually best be done elsewhere. Benefits other than protection which are available with the insurance are secondary and usually expensive as compared to alternative approaches. Shopping for insurance is not easy. It is probably more difficult to compare the various policies which different companies offer than it is to compare similar cars from different manufacturers. But the increased benefits and savings are well worth the time you devote to the task.

Amount of Insurance to Buy

Determining the amount of life insurance you need is not as difficult as it may appear. First, any determination should be made based on the prospect of imminent death. That is, if you died today, how much money from insurance would your family need. This can be done in one or both of two ways. You could conduct a hypothetical probate of your estate as of this date. You can find resource books in your public library to assist you. Additionally, you can estimate the amount of immediate cash your family survivors will need and determine ongoing income they will need from invested funds. Then subtract existing money which would be available from your estate for investing. The results will be the amount of additional life insurance, if any, you need to purchase.

The question is often asked about the need for life insurance on the wife and children. For the wife, the answer would be yes if she is a wage earner or if there are still young children in the home. The amount should be based on the existing need for the family. The need will likely diminish in direct proportion to age: the closer a couple comes to retirement, the less the need for life insurance for the wife or husband.

There may be some justification for life insurance for children. The premiums are much less when purchased for a very young child. It is one way of saving for college costs, but certainly not the best way. (If the premiums were invested instead, the return would be much greater.) Probably the strongest argument is to guarantee insurability. But even this argument is rather weak. According to the Institute of Life Insurance, 92 percent of the people who apply for insurance are accepted at regular rates. Also, guaranteed insurability is often for amounts as low as $5,000 which is almost an insignificant amount for an adult with a family.

Estate Planning

Estate planning is a broad term. It involves the careful organization of one's affairs and planned distribution of real and personal property. One purpose of estate planning is to transfer ownership of one's wealth to other persons or causes with the greatest accuracy and expediency, and with minimum depletion of the estate.

Estate planning can be a creative activity for Christians. When there is a desire to image God with the resources he has provided for our use, planning for the final distribution of our wealth may be an opportunity to support Christian ministries and help others more than ever. It may be that through estate planning we can give more for Christian ministries at death than during our entire lifetime. This kind of giving may be possible and still provide adequately for your family. Even being able to provide for your family after death is a rewarding possibility. Sometimes, a charitable gift can actually increase the amount left for the family.

You Have an Estate

Most every person has two estates: a living estate and a death estate. If you have furniture, house, car, a life insurance policy, or other real and personal property, you have an estate. Management of the living estate consists mainly of financial planning. But the same property will usually be involved in your death estate, also. Though estate planning can provide benefits to a person during his or her lifetime, the emphasis is on the death estate.

One of the major differences in the living and death estates involves life insurance. While you are alive, the value of life insurance to your estate is only its cash value. Depending on how long the policy has been in force and the face value which helps determine the amount of premiums you pay, the cash value may be very little. If it is term life insurance, there is usually no cash value. But when you die, the face value of life insurance policies less any loans, if any, against them become a part of your estate.

To arrange for management of your estate is the main purpose of estate planning. To begin, you must know what your estate contains. This means taking an inventory. Most people I know dislike inventorying their estate as much as any other kind of inventory. It is a tedious, time-consuming chore. But when a thorough inventory is completed, you will have determined the net worth of your estate. There are many books with forms and suggestions available for you to use. Your public library probably contains numerous books on estate planning. (The notes for this chapter list some of the books that may be available.)

When I first began to study and practice money management, I did not appreciate the value of determining my net worth. Later I discovered that there are two important reasons for it. First, in the event of your death, particularly accidental, a current inventory of your estate would be of great value to your spouse (executor/executrix) or administrator. It saves time, agony, and expenses for your heirs. When current information is provided about life insurance, for example, your family can file for claims immediately. Through the preparation of a net worth statement, you might discover that there would not be enough liquid assets available to pay for last expenses (assets which can be converted to money quickly). To discover and correct such a situation could prevent much anguish, inconvenience, and prevent a part of your estate from having to be sold too quickly and for too little.

The second good reason for having an up-to-date net worth statement applies more to large estates. When an estate reaches a value against which estate taxes will be levied it, this information needs to be known promptly. With current estate information, an attorney who specializes in estate planning can help you avoid unnecessary taxes and probate costs. Whatever the size of the estate, such planning is good money management and good Christian stewardship.

Keep Up with Changes

Since the Economic Recovery Act of 1981, federal estate tax laws have been greatly liberalized.

> In most cases, there is no longer need for trusts to shelter assets or to defer or to avoid taxes. Unless a married couple is relatively well-to-do . . . (roughly a net worth of $400,000 in 1985 and $600,000 by 1987) . . . there should be no federal taxes on the estate of the first to die. But there can still be substantial levies on the same assets at the death of the surviving spouse.[3]

The part of the tax law which has eliminated federal estate and gift taxes for at least 90 percent of the population is the unlimited marital deduction. This means that trusts are now more advantageous in special situations such as aid to children or grandchildren and dependent relatives, and to make gifts or to save taxes on the estate of the surviving spouse. (Congress often changes tax laws. It is the individual's responsibility to find out how changes will affect them and revise estate plans accordingly. Often, qualified estate planners will need to be consulted.)

In essence, the Economic Recovery Act of 1981 defers taxes until the second spouse dies. This is a welcomed revision in the estate tax laws, but it can be misleading. When the joint estate of a husband and wife becomes the estate of the surviving spouse, it can become sizable and subject to a higher tax rate at the survivor's death. As some have observed,

> The changes made by the Act will effectively eliminate estate and gift taxes for the vast majority of individuals. Although this may reduce the need for estate tax planning, there is an increased need for other planning for the orderly transfer of property between family members. In addition, there may be a tendency to take advantage of the full marital deduction to avoid estate and gift taxes. This may increase the estate tax of the surviving spouse. This increase in tax may be minimized or eliminated through proper estate planning for the family unit.[4]

For example, a middle-income family may appear only to have a house as the major asset in its estate. The husband has $50,000 life insurance to pay off the house mortgage at his death. But his company also provides $100,000 life insurance for him. Since he travels for the company, another $100,000 accidental death insurance is provided. When making travel arrangements, the travel agency which the company uses provides accidental death coverage of $100,000. The $50,000 life insurance policy the husband carries has an accidental death rider on it which doubles its face value. If the husband of this middle-income family should be killed accidentally, his wife could have an estate of about $400,000. With provisions for a trust, many tax dollars could be saved at the wife's death.

Other misleading aspects of the Economic Recovery Act should also be considered. The unlimited marital deduction is of no benefit to those who are single and those who are already widows or widowers. Also remember that it applies only to federal estate taxes and gifts. A person must always consider state and local tax laws. However, some state tax laws have or are being amended similarly. The need for Christians to do estate planning is as great as ever.

"Estate planning should start with broad objectives and then narrow to specific projects and terms. It should be sufficiently flexible to be expanded, contracted, and revised."[5] Estate planning should be started as soon as you have accumulated any type of property. Your program should be reviewed frequently and revised when there are major changes in your life or livelihood—children, divorce, death in the family, illness, dependent relatives, a new position, or a move to another state. Changes in federal or state laws may also call for a revision. In estate planning, "time is your powerful ally, so do take an inventory now and get started."[6]

Wills

The first essential action a Christian should take in estate planning is making a will. It is so simple to do but so valuable. It is a powerful way to demonstrate both your love and compassion for your family and your Christian commitment. For a Christian to die without a will (intestate) is very near to denouncing concern for one's family and Christ's mission in the world. Only to those who have never heard or who have been badly misinformed about making a will would I apologize for such a strong statement. What you do with your estate is an extension of your commitment and life-style.

It is extremely unfortunate that 70 percent of those who should have a will do not have one. Of the remaining 30 percent, one-third of them are out-of-date when they are brought to probate court.[7] Gordon Caswell also notes that "80 percent of those who do have a . . . will . . . have not taken advantage of approved tax plans to preserve their estates."[8] Women and singles are the greatest procrastinators.

Your Will and Estate Planning

A properly drawn will is the primary instrument to use in arranging your estate. It can be a comprehensive, written, legal description for the distribution of your real and personal property. Since every estate, including yours, must be settled by law, it is your Christian responsibility to make the decisions while you are competent. Being in charge of material things as assigned by God includes making these final decisions and expressing them in a will.

As in all estate planning, the family life cycle will influence the distribution of your estate. When your family is young, your will should usually concentrate on provisions for the family. This is especially true when minor children are involved. In your will, you can name a guardian for your dependent children. Husband and wife will likely want to make reciprocal wills and name each other as guardian. But each will should also name an alternate guardian in the event both parents die in a common accident.

Your will is used to name the executor of your estate. In reciprocal wills, each spouse can name the other; but as with the guardian, an alternate executor should be named. This executor does not have to be the guardian for your children. In fact, it may be best to name another person. To be completely sure of having someone responsible for your estate, you may also wish to name a coexecutor. The coexecutor could be an institution such as a foundation or bank trust department whose continuing existence doesn't depend upon one person.

It is obvious that your will should undergo several revisions during your lifetime. There is wisdom in reviewing it annually, even if you are not aware of a need for changes. But at each change in the life cycle it needs to actually be revised: when children are born, reach maturity, marry, become disabled, or when parents become disabled or die. Changes in vocation, income, real and personal property, retirement, a spouse's death, and other changes also signal the need to revise your will. A move to another state creates an urgent need to revise your will because state laws differ so widely.

Facts About Wills

The term probate needs to be understood.—It means "to prove." When referring to a will, "probate is a general term used to signify the administration and distribution of property belonging to the deceased. More specifically, probate is a legal process that carries out the provisions of a person's will or, if there is no will, adheres to the laws concerning the distribution of such property."[9]

- If you die without a will (intestate), your estate will be probated according to state statutes used for distributing your estate with no regard to your wishes.
- For probate, in most states, legal counsel is needed to represent the executor. Then . . .
- The court is petitioned for a hearing on the will.
- The estate is appraised.

- Creditors have six months to make claims on the estate.
- State and federal inheritance tax returns must be filed within nine months unless the estate is small enough to be exempt.
- Finally, when all taxes and claims against the estate have been satisfied, the judge signs a final decree of distribution.
- All of this long process costs money. Probate will usually cost between 2 and 5 percent of the estate, depending on its size. Most of the cost is for legal and executor's fees.
- The better the planning and the clearer the intent of the will, the less the cost.

Joint tenancy does not prevent needing a will.—"The manner in which property is owned is most meaningful for estate planning purposes."[10] It is true; in the 1981 Economic Recovery Act, joint ownership is assumed for separate property states as well as those in community property states, but . . .

- You cannot put everything in joint tenancy.
- Without a will, the spouse may only get one half or one third and the children will get the rest depending on the state.
- Joint tenancy often provides no money for liabilities.
- Without a will, an administrator will be appointed by the court.
- A will makes changing legal ownership names easier and less complicated.
- Joint tenancy does not work if both spouses die in a common accident.

You need to know if you live in a community property state.—At this writing those states are: Arizona, California, Idaho, Louisiana, Nevada, New Mexico, Texas, and Washington.

- In community property states when there are children, a will is usually essential if you want your half of the estate to go to your spouse.
- All property is considered to be owned equally.
- Gifts and inheritances, etc., require proof of separate ownership.
- Community property states present unique needs in drawing a will and in estate planning. It can be particularly complicated if property is owned in another state or if you do not live in but have property in a community property state.

You cannot do some things in a will in some states.

- You cannot disinherit a spouse (or children) in most states.
- Bequests to charities are usually invalid unless made thirty days or more before death.

In your will:

- Use percentages, be specific, name an executor, consider taxes, make no assumptions, keep the will as simple as possible, and be cautious about using codicils (changes made in a will by attaching a document without rewriting the will) and letters of intent (nonlegal instructions attached to the will after the will is prepared).
- Destroy old will when you sign a new one.

When you are preparing to make a will:

- Provide your lawyer with accurate, well-organized information, and clear guidelines.

- Choose an attorney who is familiar with writing wills. Your family or business attorney may or may not be qualified.

And remember: "Four times as many families *without* a will quarrel as families *with* a will"[11] when the estate of a decedent must be settled.

Trusts

As noted earlier, the value of trusts for the first spouse to die was greatly diminished by the 1981 Economic Recovery Tax Act which raised by annual stages the limits for taxable estates to $600,000 by 1987. This was actually accomplished by raising the Unified Tax Credit shown in the following illustration.

Year	Unified Tax Credit	Taxable Estate
1981	$47,000	$175,625
....	......	......
1984	96,000	325,000
1985	121,000	400,000
1986	155,800	500,000
1987	192,800	600,000

Trusts can still be useful, especially charitable trusts when used by Christians. They are helpful for both living and afterdeath goals. In setting up any kind of trust, however, wise counsel is needed from professionals in the field of estate planning.

"A trust is a written legal document whereby assets are turned over to someone else to hold and manage for the benefit of a third party."[12] In other words, a trust is based on a relationship which exists when an owner transfers property to a trustee who must use the assets exclusively for the benefit of the beneficiary(ies) named. The beneficiary-(ies) may or may not include the owner himself.

Characteristics of a Trust

Usually the benefits of a trust to an individual or family results in the ability to:

- Minimize taxes: on income while living, on estates after death though this has lessened since the Economic Recovery Act of 1981.
- Assure that your wishes with regard to your assets will be carried out—occasionally while you live and certainly after you die.
- Provide a flexible means of administration and accommodation to changes unforeseen at the time the trust was entered into.
- Avoid the necessity of probate for some of your assets.
- Keep some assets out of the hands of creditors.
- Assure privacy of assets.
- Permit the retention of professional assistance.

Categories of Trusts

Different trusts can be divided into living or testamentary and subdivided into revocable or irrevocable.

Living Trusts.—Basically, a living trust makes it possible to provide management continuity and income flow even after you die. No probate is necessary since the trust continues to operate after you die or provides for the manner in which assets are to be distributed.

The second advantage of a living trust is that the burdens of investment decisions and management responsibility may be taken from your shoulders and assumed by your trustee. You may want to control investment decisions and management policy as long as you are alive and healthy, but you may want to set up a trust to provide backup help in case you become unable or unwilling to manage your assets. The disadvantage is that this costs money.

Some benefits of a living trust are:

- The cost of probate and administration fees saved because the trust assets are not probated through the courts.
- The prolonged probate time can be saved, as the assets can be passed immediately. All creditors must be paid, and the federal estate taxes and the state taxes can be put into an escrow account with the trustee liable.
- The problem of incapacity is lessened.
- The trust can afford privacy in death as to the amount of the assets held in the estate, since it does not go through probate.
- A trust can keep the estate under family control.

Living trusts can be revocable or irrevocable. Irrevocable trusts should be entered into carefully since they may create special tax problems. The property involved is considered a gift and thus not subject to estate taxes. The beneficiary pays the taxes on distributed income. Short-term trusts are a form of irrevocable trust that run for at least ten years or the lifetime of the beneficiary. This can be valuable when contributing to the support of an elderly parent.

Charitable Trusts.—They are gifts to charitable institutions that enable you to "give while you live." They provide current income tax deductions, lower estate taxes, avoid capital gains taxes, and generally distribute income for the grantor. Charitable trusts may be revocable or irrevocable. They are usually one of three types: charitable remainder annuity trust, charitable remainder unitrust, or pooled income fund. Each one provides certain benefits because of their differences.

Testamentary Trusts.—The widest use of testamentary trusts is to help avoid future estate tax levies against the property. It is set up by a person's will and does not become operative until after the death of the creator. There are no income tax savings because property is not given until death.

However, a trust does shift the burdens of asset management and investment decisions from your beneficiaries to the trustee. It also can be used to delay or control the distribution of assets—who receives what, when, and how much. Good examples are when beneficiaries are minors, spendthrifts, and mental or emotional incompetents. These people need asset management for obvious reasons. This is a particularly good way to provide income for needy parents without giving up a part or all of your estate. After their need passes, the corpus of the trust could be returned to you or given to some other person. Often a charitable trust is used for this purpose.

The greatest advantage for Christians in using trusts is not saving tax money for themselves. Tax benefits should never be placed above personal or family needs. The real measure of a worthwhile trust is not cost or assets; it is purpose. Christians can often exercise more control for contributing to Christian causes when using trusts.

Conclusion

I have not tried in any way to be comprehensive in dealing with all of the subject areas of planning for the future. Even the subjects discussed are embarrassingly sketchy. My intent is to create awareness for the responsibility Christians need to assume in this area. Professional people and books are available to assist you personally.

In the Prologue, I confessed my many years of illiteracy

about God's management principles. It became apparent
that I was not alone in my ignorance. But illiteracy is not
confined to biblical understanding; it includes contemporary
economic/financial matters. Sylvia Porter notes that "we are
a nation of economic illiterates."[13] VanCaspel also writes,

> I'm saddened to see how many uninformed and frightened
> people are still trying to cope with a subject for which they
> have received absolutely no training. Our educational sys-
> tem continues to send forth our young with so little informa-
> tion about financial matters that they are like time bombs
> about to destroy their own and their families' economic fu-
> ture.[14]

I agree with these financial counselors and planners.
Though most Christians live good moral lives which have
contributed greatly to the advance of Christianity in the
world, their impact has been greatly diminished because of
mismanagement. Lack of understanding and ability to live
effectively in our contemporary economic/financial society
is a continuous reminder of Christians' management challenge. Money is certainly not everything, but it is a valuable
tool in the hands of Christians to enlarge God's kingdom on
earth.

Notes

1. Venita VanCaspel, *The Power of Money Dynamics* (Reston: Virginia: Reston Publishing Company, 1983), p. 436.

2. *Current Social Issues: The Public's View* (Washington: American Council of Life
Insurance), pamphlet.

3. C. Colburn Hardy, *Your Guide to a Financially Secure Retirement* (New York: Harper
& Row, Publishers, 1983), p. 163.

4. *The Economic Recovery Tax Act of 1981.* Peat, Marwick, Mitchell & Company,
August 5, 1981.

5. C. Colburn Hardy, *Your Money and Your Life; Planning Your Financial Future* (Second
edition, New York: Amacom, 1982), p. 245.

6. VanCaspel, p. 462.

7. Hardy, *Your Money and Your Life,* p. 275.

8. Gordon M. Caswell and Associates, "Annual and Deferred Gifts Institute," 1978, p. 1.

9. Hardy, *Your Money and Your Life,* p. 259.

10. Robert S. Holzman, *Encyclopedia of Estate Planning* (New York: Boardroom Books, Inc., 1981), p. 104.

11. Hardy, *Your Life and Your Money,* p. 260

12. Hardy, *Your Money and Your Life,* p. 247.

13. Sylvia Porter, *Sylvia Porter's New Money Book for the 80's* (New York: Avon Books, 1979), p. 1269.

14. VanCaspel, p. 436.

Postscript
Our Continuing Pilgrimage

Reflecting upon and recording my family's pilgrimage in Christian money management has been totally reaffirming. The new research in preparation for writing this book has been a joy and very rewarding for me. My understanding of and commitment to the biblical doctrine of management has become clearer and more focused. But what has become most obvious is the management excellence not yet achieved. I wrote in the Prologue that the only Christians I know who are serious about money management are those who are still working at it. I really didn't realize the significance those words would have for me by the time I finished.

In these last few pages, I want to suggest some ideas for our continuing pilgrimage in Christian money management. The ideas are in three categories: personal, family, and church.

Continuing Personal Growth

Continue to refine your money management skills.—If intentional money management is a new experience for you, you'll become proficient with practice. The excitement will build as you observe your progress each time you "do the books." (That's the term we use for the weekly recording of deposits and expenditures.) You will likely notice a gradual increase in your net worth and be able to give thanks for God's provisions and for the biblical doctrine of management.

You'll likely experience the thrill of being able to do more in God's kingdom work.

Continue to study.—Study will help keep you sensitive to God's leadership in your life. Every biblical truth you discover, when put into practice in your life, is a management (stewardship) application. The resources referenced in this book would provide weeks of study for you, maybe years. There are many other books available on money management from which you can gain helpful information. Check with your nearest public library.

Explore the possibility of developing a simpler life-style.—Richard Foster, a theology professor and writer, quotes G. K. Chesterton: "There are two ways to get enough: one is to continue to accumulate more and more. The other is to desire less."[1] It's not necessary to join a monastery, convent, or commune to live a simpler life. Though an intentional choice to live a simpler life is somewhat countercultural, it doesn't have to be otherworldly. It can just be a conscious decision to not be manipulated by the success images promoted through advertising and commercial culture. Obviously, the more simply we live, the less goods and services we'll need. This will reduce the drain on natural resources and free more money for Christian mission ministries. I like the concept of striving to live a life of creative simplicity.

There are many books available on the subject of simple living which I encourage you to locate and study.

Adopt a world view.—We can't live an isolated life in our corner of the world; God never intended that we should. Hunger, conflicts, and war in any part of the world eventually affect us. (Remember the Middle East oil embargo?) Christ's Great Commission (Matt. 28:19-20) makes us responsible for the spiritual condition of the world's people. Christ's many other teachings hold us responsible for the physical condition of all people.

Become involved in ecological concerns, conservation, and recycling.
—In the spirit of a manager in charge of God's world, guard
and protect the environment and natural resources. Look for
ways to recycle materials. Any kind of recycling is good
management because it conserves resources and reduces pollution. We need to develop a tough-mindedness about all
management that affects the environment and natural resources of our world, and we should support those who are
trying to make the tough decisions for the future.

Continuing Emphasis on Management in the Family

Management strengthens families.—I'm more convinced than
ever that understanding and applying Christian management principles in the home will make a major contribution
to the strength of families. Pastoral counselor Paul Schurman writes: "There is a close tie between economics and
family stability. The state of the economy and the well-
being of the home go hand in hand."[2] Schurman also notes
how instability in the economy breeds a sense of powerless-
ness in families. This causes conflict between spouses and
children. Management principles applied in the home
become a stabilizing factor giving families optimism and
hope.

*Management in the home is one of the better ways of transferring
family values to our children.*—If we want our children to learn
music, we provide lessons. Whatever our dreams are for our
children, we parents will go to all lengths to provide the
necessary background and training. But too often our children are ill-prepared to function as managers of God's
world. Management skills are most needed and less taught.
Our children will need management skills almost every
waking hour of their adult lives. Edwin Graham, director of
Education and Community Services, American Council of

Life Insurance, notes that only one percent of seventeen-year-olds know how to balance a checkbook.[3]

But maybe more important than teaching our children how to balance a checkbook (though that's important) is teaching them how to live. Basic attitudes and life-style patterns are learned in the home.

The Church Teaching Management

We need to make up for lost time.—Until at the age of thirty-six I started teaching biblical management principles in the church, I can't recall hearing of the subject. All I ever heard taught about stewardship before then was giving. Theologian Francis Schaeffer writes:

> Man has dominion over nature, but he uses it wrongly. The Christian is called upon to exhibit this dominion, but exhibit it rightly: treating the thing as having value in itself, exercising dominion without being destructive. The church should always have taught and done this, but she generally failed to do so, and we need to confess our failure.[4]

Not only do we need to confess our failure, we need to excel in our opportunities and responsibilities to teach Christians biblical management principles for living. Teaching Christian money management can provide a foundation for all other management teachings.

I have found the following ideas helpful in planning and teaching money management in the church.—Preparation includes deciding how many sessions to have. Basically, the number of sessions depends upon the objective. The record-keeping part of money management can be explained in a one-hour session. But teaching record keeping should not be the primary purpose of planning a money management seminar. Hopefully the emphasis will be on nurturing Christians, equipping them to live and minister as Christian disciples. When management of resources is taught, it needs a biblical/theological foundation. (Note the arrangement of this book. It is in the format of the conferences I lead.)

Ideally, an extended number of sessions will be planned which includes both the biblical/theological foundation and practical application. Six one-hour sessions (or fifty minutes usually) will provide time for presentation and discussion.

Session one	Biblical/theological foundation
Session two	Christian life-style
Session three	Goals and income
Session four	Expenses and plan for spending
Session five	Records
Session six	Planning for the future

Variations of this format are easily accommodated. For example, sessions four and five can be comfortably combined into session four. Then sessions five and six can be used for more specific topics such as estate planning, making a will (which is a part of estate planning), and/or investments.

Scheduling is another important part of planning. The first time money management is taught in a church it is usually best to schedule it at the time of an ongoing church activity. There is a stigma attached to anything to do with money, except making more of it. Members are afraid that they will be pressured to do something they don't want to do, that a money management conference at church (of all places) must be a veiled scheme to separate members from more of their money unwillingly. But don't be too hard on others. The only experience many of them have had at church related to money was about their giving more. A money management conference scheduled at the time of an ongoing church activity will usually reach at least the faithful.

In scheduling, consider providing a group(s) for youth. I would like to suggest that children also be included, but at present the only material I know of for children is out of print. We tend to have a mind-set that since adults pay the bills, they are the ones to reach in money matters. But we need to teach youth and children how to be Christian managers before they learn management the wrong way.

Who should be the leader? An interested, dedicated layperson capable of learning the material is better than a professional in the field of money but who is only a nominal Christian. A person who approaches money management as a professional without a commitment to and an understanding of Christian management can do much more harm than good. However, many churches have members who are professionals in the field and who are dedicated Christians. Use them, by all means.

Promotion and publicity need a special touch. Just announcing a money management conference probably won't get results. Though a money management conference is not just for those who are having financial problems, many will interpret it that way. It is best to enlist two or three couples and preview the conference agenda with them. Help them to see the value and nature of it. Then ask them to enlist other couples (or individuals) personally. General promotion and publicity does need to be done—posters, articles in the newsletter, and other ways—because someone very interested in learning more about money management might be overlooked in the personal contact approach.

Materials are available from various sources. Those I'm most familiar with may be obtained from the following sources: SBC Stewardship Services, 901 Commerce Street, Nashville, Tennessee 37203. An SBC *Stewardship Services Catalog* may be obtained at this address which describes the materials. In particular, the catalog lists a "Christian Family

Money Management Packet" (FS-B) which includes a sample of most materials available, adult and youth. Apart from the packet, there is a filmstrip, *Christian Money Management Day-by-Day,* which is designed to be used with the *Christian Family Money Management* workbook (FS-1). The workbook is in the packet and sold separately.

Other materials are available from Material Services, Baptist Sunday School Board, 127 Ninth Avenue, North, Nashville, Tennessee 37234. Two equipping center modules are available from Material Services: *A Christian's Guide to Financial Planning* and *The Bible Speaks on Stewardship.*

Christian Family Money Management (4460-29) is a 16-minute videocassette which introduces the biblical concept of management and reviews the materials available. Southern Baptist churches may obtain this videocassette on loan from most Baptist state convention offices, rent it from one of the Baptist Film Centers, or purchase it from Broadman Consumer Sales, Nashville, Tennessee 37234.

Notes

1. Richard J. Foster, *Freedom of Simplicity* (San Francisco: Harper & Row, 1973), p. 110.

2. Paul G. Schurman. *Money Problems and Pastoral Care,* Creative Pastoral Care and Counseling Series, ed. Howard J. Clinebell (Philadelphia: Fortress Press, 1982), p. 3.

3. Edwin K. Graham, Lecture before the Large Church Stewardship Conference, Lakeway Resort, Austin, Texas, February 27-March 1, 1978.

4. Francis A. Schaeffer. *Pollution and the Death of Man* (Wheaton, Illinois: Tyndale House, 1970), p. 72.